Charisma

Perform with power. Connect with confidence.

- Nelson Mandela
- Johnny Depp
- Princess Diana
- Bill Clinton
- Muhammad Ali

David Gillespie and Mark Warren

For UK order enquiries: please contact Bookpoint Ltd, 130 Milton Park, Abingdon, Oxon OX14 4SB. Telephone: +44 (0) 1235 827720. Fax: +44 (0) 1235 400454. Lines are open 09.00–17.00, Monday to Saturday, with a 24-hour message answering service. Details about our titles and how to order are available at www.hoddereducation.com

British Library Cataloguing in Publication Data: a catalogue record for this title is available from the British Library.

First published in UK 2011 by Hodder Education, part of Hachette UK, 338 Euston Road, London NW1 3BH.

Copyright © 2011 David Gillespie and Mark Warren

Typeset by MPS Limited, a Macmillan Company.

Printed and bound by CPI Group (UK) Ltd, Croydon, CR0 4YY.

Cover design by D.R.ink

The publisher has used its best endeavours to ensure that the URLs for external websites referred to in this book are correct and active at the time of going to press. However, the publisher and the author have no responsibility for the websites and can make no guarantee that a site will remain live or that the content will remain relevant, decent or appropriate.

Hachette UK's policy is to use papers that are natural, renewable and recyclable products and made from wood grown in sustainable forests. The logging and manufacturing processes are expected to conform to the environmental regulations of the country of origin.

Impression number 10 9 8 7 6 5 4 3 2

Year 2015 2014 2013 2012 2011

Acknowledgements

The authors would like to thank the following for their invaluable help and assistance: Alison Frecknall, Dan Kirkby, Charles Parsons, Nigel Pritchard, Hillary Wood, Jim Dunk, Liz Earle, Michael Brooke, Georgie Gulliford, Tessa Wood, Chris Cramer, Jeremy Thompson, Melanie Jessop, Bruce Priday, Dr Victoria Hill, Dennis K. Hoffert, Major-General Andy Salmon CMG OBE, Reverend Ruth Scott, Louise Goodman, Arne L. Schmidt, Trish Lynch, Laura Hilliard, Dai Taylor, Laura Davis, Gail Blanke, Victoria Roddam and Sam Richardson.

About the Authors and The Speechworks

The actor, David Gillespie and writer, Mark Warren have many acting and writing credits between them in TV, film and theatre. They are also partners in The Speechworks, which specializes in presentation skills and communication skills training for board directors, senior executives, public figures and sports personalities. Training is one-to-one and in small groups. Their blue-chip client list includes global companies, professional bodies, charities, government departments and public sector services.

Every member of The Speechworks team is a professional actor, director or writer with many years' experience of working in film, TV and theatre. They teach the skills and techniques that are the performers' tools of the trade and show clients how to use them with confidence.

The Speechworks
Leaders in communication skills and presentation skills training
www.thespeechworks.co.uk

Contents

Part 01: Charisma

Chapters:

Part 02: Introducing Story, Status and Focus – the keys to communicating with charisma

Chapters:

Part 03: Communicating with charisma – Story

Chapters:

Part 04: Communicating with charisma – Status

Chapters:

Part 05: Communicating with charisma – Focus

Chapters:

Part 06: Communicating with charisma – Story, Status, Focus

Forewords

Chris Cramer, former President, CNN International

I am sure many of us have been there and I'm not sure that either time or advanced age is a great healer.

I refer to the sheer terror caused by an impending speech, a presentation to colleagues or clients, a wedding speech as Best Man or Friend of the Bride, or – much worse – an oration delivered at a funeral in honour of a departed loved one.

They say that public speaking is our number one fear. The sleepless nights, the days of anguish, the body sweats just before we reach the podium. I had a friend who, on frequent occasions, vomited before he took to the stage. I myself have fainted at least twice waiting in the wings. And let's not forget those poor souls who have sometimes resorted to 'fight or flight' prescription drugs to get them through the ordeal.

On the other hand, there are those who appear effortless as they address the world. Those brilliant public speakers who are able to stride purposefully to the podium, remove a single sheet of paper from their pocket, smile broadly and, within minutes, have us eating out of their hands. We are entranced by their eloquence. In awe of their oratory.

Life can seem so unfair.

This book lifts the lid on the art of brilliant communication. It does so by focusing on some of the best communicators of our time; Sir Winston Churchill, Martin Luther King, President John F. Kennedy,

Nelson Mandela, and one of my favourites, Colonel Tim Collins of the Royal Irish Regiment, who sent his men into battle in Iraq in 2003 with the kind of speech that you imagine Julius Caesar gave his Roman legions. The kind of speech that chills your spine and raises your soul.

This book is about the skills and expertise we may have and about translating them into a narrative – a story – that other people might care to listen to. It's about the great communicators and how we can all begin to learn how to communicate with charisma.

It reminds us early on that the best communicators edit their presentations and edit them again, and then again. So let me do so.

This is a great book. Keep reading.

Gail Blanke

Curtain up!

Okay, most of us aren't dying to stand up in front of people and talk. In fact, according to the List of Greatest Fears, public speaking ranks above dying. So I guess that means we'd rather die than get up there and talk …

Even the most accomplished among us gets 'worked up'. As we began working on a major speech she was about to give in front of thousands of people, an extremely high-powered executive from a Fortune 50 company said, 'I've got an idea, Gail, you do the talking and I'll move my mouth. Just think, it'll be the first lip-synched speech in history!'

But seriously, there's never been a time when it was more vital or more critical to be able to communicate, to make one's voice heard, to move people to action, to *lead*. At the core, a leader is someone who has the passion and the courage to stand up, stand out, and stand for ... a vision of what's possible and the ability to motivate others to join forces to bring it to life. Leaders inspire ordinary people to discover the courage to be bold, to use themselves fully and to create miracles. And yet that ability, that skill, that visible energy, seems to be sorely lacking, in countries, in companies, in communities – even in families.

But not for long. All that will change. David Gillespie and Mark Warren have created a world-class compendium of the best-of-breed (and most entertaining) advice for unraveling the mysteries of magnetism and presenting it as a gift for the reader to delight in – and learn from.

And here's more good news: in terms of charisma? *You've already got it.* And these guys will show you how to tap into it. My dad always told me that charisma was 'passion demonstrated'. David and Mark show you how to uncover your passion for what's possible and craft a story that will move people. (Never underestimate the power of a story. In the end, we are nothing more or less than the stories we make up about ourselves ... and believe.) They'll also show you how to develop a voice that captivates and a physical presence that owns the room. And perhaps most importantly, they'll convince you that the most powerful and unforgettable communicators in the world are the greatest listeners.

Will it require some work on your part? Yes. Can you do it? Yes. Will there be a review in the future that describes *you* as 'charismatic?' For sure.

Okay, so this is your moment. Are you ready? There's the drumroll and they're playing your song. Start reading.

Gail Blanke is a best selling author of four books. Her latest is Throw Out Fifty Things; Clear the Clutter, Find Your Life. *A renowned executive coach and presentation skills trainer, Gail has advised CEOs presidential candidates, college presidents and stand-up comics.*

Major-General Andy Salmon CMG OBE, former Commandant-General Royal Marines

The art of effective communication is looking, listening, thinking and choosing the right language to create the desired effect – this book does exactly that!

Part
01

Charisma

When I left the dining room after sitting next to Mr. Gladstone, I thought he was the cleverest man in England. But after sitting next to Mr. Disraeli, I thought I was the cleverest woman in England.

How someone responded when asked her impression of the two English statesmen Benjamin Disraeli and William Gladstone after dining with them.

Thank you for leaving us alone but giving us enough attention to boost our egos.

Mick Jagger

1

Communicating with charisma

Sometimes one creates a dynamic impression by saying something, and sometimes one creates as significant an impression by remaining silent.

Dalai Lama

Charisma – get what the greats have got – wouldn't that be something? To have appeal. To be attractive. To have people wanting to be in our company. To have others seeking our advice and our opinion. To be popular. To be wanted for whom we are, not for what we have. To be respected and liked.

All of us would like to be able to communicate with charisma, wouldn't we?

In fact, enhancing our communicating abilities with charisma is something that we would all really love to be able to do. But just how do we go about doing it? How do we get what the greats have got?

Surely, you may say, the greats, those who we recognize as being able to communicate with charisma, were born with this special talent, this skill, this magic. And we lesser mortals were not. Well, yes and no. It's true that some of the world's great communicators seemed to have a natural gift for it. Charisma and being able to communicate with charisma were part of their DNA.

But we believe that all human beings have a certain personal charisma that we can tap into and develop. It may not occur to all of us that we have this charisma. We may not be aware of it, but it is there. If we want to be successful and get the best out of life it's vital that we know how to communicate well. To communicate with others powerfully, persuasively and effectively we must develop our personal appeal, our charm, our charisma. The vast majority of successful people have a certain charisma, and they use that appeal and attractiveness to further their ambitions and desires.

Truly charmless people, on the other hand, are seldom successful in anything that requires interpersonal communication. These people are few and very far between, and generally keep themselves away from the rest of us. So let's concentrate on the majority of us and focus on what we need to do to tap into our charisma and develop it further.

We need to believe that our charisma is already there, waiting to be developed. There will always be those who seem to exude 'natural' charisma. There are numbered among those 'naturals' those who have recognized what they have and sought to develop it further. There are many who, in order to create a following, have acknowledged the need to enhance their charismatic power. There are many great speakers and communicators who have not always been as good as they are now – they have been the smart ones who looked for help to develop their personal skills. Whether it is natural, cultivated or a mixture of both, being able to communicate with charisma is an undeniably attractive quality.

For all of us there have been times when we have made someone else smile or laugh. There have been times when someone has come to us for advice or assurance. And there have been times when someone has confided in us, and times when someone has simply put his or her head on our shoulder and sobbed.

These moments would not have happened if those people did not feel drawn to us as a person. That draw or pull is something that we all have in varying degrees. Those very words 'draw' and 'pull' are often associated with magnetism, and magnetism is always linked to charisma.

But what do we understand by the word charisma? We recognize it in individuals and we know its power. But what does it actually mean?

2

What is charisma?

With my sunglasses on, I'm Jack Nicholson. Without them, I'm fat and 60.

Jack Nicholson

The dictionary definitions of charisma make interesting reading.

The *Chambers Concise Dictionary* defines charisma as: 'A strong ability to attract people, and inspire loyalty and admiration' (*Chambers Concise Dictionary*, 2nd edition, 2009).

Other definitions include:

● A special personal quality or power of an individual making him capable of influencing or inspiring large numbers of people.

● A quality inherent in a thing which inspires great enthusiasm and devotion.

- *Charisma* a divinely bestowed power or talent (Christianity/ecclesiastical terms).

- A rare personal quality attributed to leaders who arouse fervent popular devotion and enthusiasm.

- Personal magnetism or charm.

In more detail, *Wikipedia* tells us that:

Charisma (meaning 'gift,' 'of/from/favoured by God/ the divine') is a trait found in individuals whose personalities are characterized by a powerful charm and magnetism (attractiveness), along with innate and markedly sophisticated abilities of interpersonal communication and persuasion. One who is charismatic is said to be capable of using their personal being, rather than just speech or logic alone, to interface with other human beings in a personal and direct manner, and effectively communicate an argument or concept to them.

The word charisma comes to us from the Greek word *kharisma*, which stems from *kharis*, meaning 'grace' or 'favour'. Its original meaning was a favour or grace or gift given by God. But the meaning of charisma now is very different.

As part of our research for this book we conducted two online surveys. In the first we asked people what they understood by the word 'charisma' and what it meant to them personally. The results were fascinating.

The question we asked was:

What's your personal definition of charisma? What does it mean to you?

Here are just some of the answers.

- It's a fancy way of saying that you can make people listen to what you have to say.

- Personal magnetism.

- The power to draw people towards you.
- Charm.
- Charisma is when you attract people by what you say and how you say it.
- Charisma comes from gifted leadership.
- The ability to inspire others.
- Someone who captivates.
- Always the centre of attention.
- It's like an aura that comes from inside and touches all the people around.
- It can't be defined but we all recognize it when we see it.
- Personal charm, influence and appeal.
- The power to attract and hold attention.
- The ability to influence by inspiring others.
- A special presence.
- A mystique that fascinates.
- The sense you get of being charmingly persuasive.
- Personal magic.
- Impossible to define.
- Amazing personal presence.
- The ability to energize with thoughts.
- Makes people sit up and listen, respond and respect.
- Communicating with passion and honesty.
- Having a vision and being able to persuade others to share that vision.
- Real charisma is being able to be true to yourself and to everyone else.
- Someone who when talking to a crowd makes everyone feel that they are being spoken to individually.
- Extrovert. Empathy. Understanding.

- Quiet but strong force of personality.
- It is difficult to differentiate charisma from leadership.
- Being able to attract attention and hold it.
- Inner clarity – outer charm.
- Exceptional interpersonal skills.
- Radiates a sense of purpose.
- It's part of leadership.

It seemed to us that everyone had a slightly different take on what charisma meant to them. But certain words and themes seemed to come up very often – attractiveness, charm, magnetism, persuasion, communication. And communication was an idea that appeared time after time after time. So, if we want to begin to 'get what the greats have got' we need to take a long hard look at our communication – how we, as individuals are communicating with others.

The opposite of charisma and how to avoid it

It's interesting to note that there is no word for the opposite of charisma. But perhaps that is not surprising. Because if charisma itself is so hard to define then this will be equally true of its opposite.

As Buddha taught: 'The mind is everything. What you think you become.'

Phrases used to describe someone who exudes the opposite of charisma (and let's be honest we've all met a few of these people) include charmless, of zero charisma, unattractive, dull, boring, lacking personality, cold and distant. Nobody wants to be thought of as a 'charisma free zone'. By using Story, Status and Focus (see Part Two) whenever we communicate with others we will be developing the inherent ability in all of us to communicate with charisma.

3

Who's got charisma?

I always knew I was a star. And now, the rest of the world seems to agree with me.

Freddie Mercury

So who do *we* the public think has charisma? Who are the greats?

For our second online survey we asked people from the worlds of business, entertainment, politics, public service and sport, to give us the names of three figures (living or dead) that they associate with charisma. We also asked them to tell us what it was about these individuals that gave them their charisma. Here are the questions we asked:

If there were Best Ever Awards for Charisma who would be your three nominees? (They can be living or dead.)

And why?

Now here are just a few of the answers we received. They not only reinforce the point that people have very different ideas of what charisma is. They also showed us that charisma is recognized as a quality in a very wide range of people.

Desmond Tutu, Placido Domingo, Mo Mowlem

Desmond Tutu – infectious energy and humour. There is no problem that cannot be addressed by harnessing our common humanity.

Placido Domingo – inspirational and respectful of all other artists no matter how young or inexperienced.

Mo Mowlem – for her passionate belief, irrepressible humour and irreverence. She had this amazing ability to win over people by being straight with people and being human.

Nelson Mandela, Bill Clinton, Desmond Tutu

Naturally trustworthy and honest, comfortable, relaxed and believable.

George Clooney, Helen Mirren, Judi Dench

They seem attractive/beautiful (inner and outer). I trust them and feel I would like them if I met them.

Richard Burton, Anthony Hopkins, Audrey Hepburn

Larger than life – massive presence – charm and grace.

David Niven, Kate Winslet, Christopher Walken

Charm and likeability. The power to draw you in.

Winston Churchill, Kevin Spacey, John F. Kennedy

Easy self-confidence, honesty and gravitas.

Nelson Mandela, William Shakespeare,
Winston Churchill

Nelson Mandela – because of the power of his social and emotional intellect.

William Shakespeare – because he presumably knew how insightful his thoughts were and in any era he would be someone you would want at your dinner party.

Winston Churchill – for the speed of his mind to say exactly the right thing in a succinct way at exactly the right time and so capture hearts and minds.

Winston Churchill, Gandhi, Nelson Mandela

These are people who could make millions of people follow them.

Cary Grant, Elizabeth I, Bill Clinton

Cary Grant – although an actor, he convinced me that if I had met him he would have had that easy and understated style which he played on screen.

Elizabeth I – to be able to hold her position and inspire loyalty as a woman in a truly man's world, she must have been an incredibly strong and eloquent communicator.

Bill Clinton – a great orator and communicator with a natural style. He edges Barack Obama who, to me least, can seem a little stiff and sterile.

David Cameron, Tony Blair, David Dimbleby

David Cameron – authenticity, transparency, ability to relate to whom he is talking to, brilliant IQ, articulate and interesting.

Tony Blair – for the same reasons as above until he lost his authenticity and the trust of his audience.

David Dimbleby – intellect, knowledge, ability to relate to those around him, genuine, fairness, perception.

Eva Peron, Ronald Reagan, Richard Branson

Eva Peron – won the hearts of a nation through her charm and determination. How many wives of politicians have had musicals written about them?

Ronald Reagan – a great communicator and actor, and one of the most popular US Presidents ever.

Richard Branson – laid-back inspirational entrepreneur and leader.

Lt.-Col. Tim Collins, Johnny Depp, Joanna Lumley

Lt.-Col. Tim Collins – gave one of the most cleverly crafted and inspirational pre-battle speeches of all time.

Johnny Depp – charmingly quiet, brilliant actor; some of the most charismatic performances I've ever seen on screen.

Joanna Lumley – campaigner and actor who brings her own brand of irresistible charm to whatever she does.

Steve Jobs, Emmeline Pankhurst, Stephen Fry

Steve Jobs – in the words of technology writer Katie Hafner '… has always had a bit of Buzz Lightyear in him: comically self-confident, ingenuously overbearing and over-endowed with charisma.'

Emmeline Pankhurst – inspired the women of Britain to campaign for what was rightfully theirs.

Stephen Fry – everyone seems to love him for his charm, wit, empathy and brain.

Freddie Mercury, George Best, Orson Welles

Freddie Mercury – had it big time and he knew it. As he once said; 'The reason we're successful, darling? My overall charisma, of course.'

George Best – womanizer, drinker, gambler; but still remembered as one of the greatest British soccer players ever to kick a ball.

Orson Welles – enigmatic, with a voice as rich as a treasure trove.

Anita Roddick, Princess Diana, Muhammad Ali

Anita Roddick – an inspiration to millions as a campaigner and activist. Successful in business, too.

Princess Diana – Earl Spencer said; '… if we look to analyse what it was about you that had such a wide appeal, we find it in your instinctive feel for what was really important in all our lives.'

Muhammad Ali – one of the most charismatic sporting figures the world has ever known.

Robin Williams, Nelson Mandela, Tony Blair

They are all superb communicators (Blair in the early years of New Labour).

Nelson Mandela, Winston Churchill, Charlie Chaplin

Why Chaplin? Because he's the only person I know who can make people listen to him without saying anything.

In the presence of charisma

Here is a first-hand account by an experienced representative of the media world of listening to a performance by an acknowledged past master of the art of communicating with charisma.

A great communicator

Bill Clinton – former President of the USA

By Jeremy Thompson, Sky News presenter

Excellent communications skills are the essence of television news. First comes the tale, then the tell. Content is King, but delivery is the Household Cavalry. It always helps to have a good story. But the key is how you get it over to people. An audience won't listen unless you're engaging, accessible, compelling and credible.

In over 30 years in TV I've seen all the latest fancy technology, new gizmos, clever graphics and glitzy studios. Not once, but many times repeated. In the end it all comes down to having a damn good yarn, looking the viewers in the eye and telling them a story they can't turn off. News hasn't changed that much since the times when town criers strode in the main square armed with no more than a bell, a strong voice and a way with words. It always has been down to the way you tell it.

Politicians aren't much different when it comes to marketing policies, persuading voters and selling dreams. Bill Clinton is the best I've ever seen. Watching him in action you knew he was born to be President. As Chief US Correspondent for Sky News in the mid 1990s, I reported on Clinton in his Washington heyday. I soon realized he was the consummate communicator. He could grab and hold your attention from two feet to 200 yards and, through television, up to 20,000 miles. He just had it. The ability to capture your attention, hold you in his sway, lead you on a journey of ideas with his words, make you believe and leave you feeling you still wanted more. He had the skill to make everyone feel that they were the only one he was speaking to when he talked – whether they were face-to-face or they were part of a vast campaign throng.

I've talked to battle-hardened TV news veterans, sceptical of his legendary charms, who admitted going weak at the knees when they were finally confronted by Bubba Bill.

I remember one particular day in Detroit during the 1996 election campaign when Clinton flew into town and addressed meeting after meeting. First it was the toughest of all blue-collar crowds on the shop floor of a car plant, who were soon cheering for Bill. Then it was on to a gathering of religious leaders of different faiths. Within minutes they were captivated and enthralled. Next, the city's captains of industry – more Republican than Democrat – but soon buying the party line. Finally it was a vast town hall meeting packed with regular voters, quickly beguiled by The Clinton Factor. In between he spoke to every small child, old lady and passing punter like he was their best pal. An extraordinary masterclass in communicating. As always, he had almost everyone rapt, spellbound, buying into Bill's message. It was like he tapped into the mains when he walked into a room and became energized by the power of the people within it. It was all about the way he used his words, wove his stories, altered his tone and changed the mood. Part-politician, part-preacher, part-storyteller but above all, a brilliant communicator.

4

Great communicators

Surround yourself with only people who are going to lift you higher.

Oprah Winfrey

As we expected the same names came up again and again in our survey – Winston Churchill, John F. Kennedy, Nelson Mandela, Barack Obama, Princess Diana, Desmond Tutu … no surprises there. But we were surprised at the sheer range of names that were suggested. So, based on the survey and on are own personal observations these are the great communicators, some of whom we will be discussing in this book. They come from the worlds of politics, sports, business, public service and entertainment, and also include famous historical figures.

Adolf Hitler
Al Pacino
Alan Rickman
Anita Roddick
Anthony Hopkins
Audrey Hepburn
Ayrton Senna
Barack Obama
Benazir Bhutto
Bill Clinton
Bill Cosby
Bill Gates
Bob Geldof
Charles De Gaulle
Charlie Chaplin
Christopher Walken
Cleopatra
Clint Eastwood
Conan O'Brien
Dalai Lama
David Bowie
David Dimbleby
David Letterman
David Niven
Desmond Tutu
Dwight D. Eisenhower
Elizabeth Taylor
Elvis Presley
Emma Thompson
Emmeline Pankhurst
Enzo Ferrari
Eric Cantona
Eric Morecambe
Eva Peron

Fidel Castro
François Pienaar
Frank Sinatra
Franklin D. Roosevelt
Freddie Mercury
General MacArthur
General Montgomery
General Patton
George Best
George Clooney
Giacomo Casanova
Giuseppe Garibaldi
Golda Meir
Graham Hill
Graham Norton
Grigori Rasputin
Helen Mirren
Henry VIII
Horatio Nelson
Indira Gandhi
Jack Nicholson
Jackie Kennedy Onassis
James Dean
Jay Leno
Jeremy Paxman
Joan of Arc
Joanna Lumley
John F. Kennedy
John Travolta
Johnny Depp
Jonathan Ross
Judi Dench
Keith Richards
Kenneth Branagh

Kevin Spacey
Larry King
Lt.-Col. Tim Collins
Luciano Pavarotti
Marcus Cicero
Marie Curie
Marilyn Monroe
Marlon Brando
Martin Luther King
Maya Angelou
Michael Caine
Michael Mansfield QC
Michael Parkinson
Mick Jagger
Mo Mowlem
Mohandas (Mahatma)
  Gandhi
Mother Teresa
Muhammad Ali
Napoleon Bonaparte
Nelson Mandela
Noel Coward
Oprah Winfrey

Orson Welles
Placido Domingo
Pope John Paul II
Princess Diana
Queen Elizabeth I
Richard Branson
Richard Burton
Richard Harris
Robert De Niro
Ronald Reagan
Samuel Goldwyn
Shirley Chisholm
Stephen Fry
Steve Jobs
Steven Spielberg
Terry Wogan
Tim Bell
Tom Cruise
Tony Curtis
Warren Buffet
William Wallace
Willie John McBride
Winston Churchill

N.B. This list is not exhaustive.

5

Charisma and emotional intelligence

I suppose leadership at one time meant muscles; but today it means getting along with people.

Mohandas Gandhi

It seems to us that charisma and the ability to communicate with charisma are closely linked to emotional intelligence.

Emotional intelligence, or EI as it is known, is the ability to perceive, control, and evaluate the emotions of both ourselves and of others.

In their article 'Emotional Intelligence' of 1990 the researchers Salovey and Mayer defined emotional intelligence as: 'The subset of social intelligence that involves the ability to monitor one's own and others' feelings and emotions, to discriminate among them and to use this information to guide one's thinking and actions.'

Further research led them to revise their definition of EI to: 'The ability to perceive emotion, integrate emotion to facilitate thought, understand emotions and to regulate emotions to promote personal growth.'

As part of this Ability EI model they identified four different factors of emotional intelligence.

1 Perception of emotion
2 Ability to reason using emotions
3 Ability to understand emotion
4 Ability to manage emotions.

The Ability EI model suggests that people vary in their ability to deal with this emotional information and use it to help in understanding.

Think of perceiving emotions as being able to detect and decode emotions in faces, voices, and body language. This includes the ability to identify our own emotions. It's the most basic aspect of emotional intelligence.

Being able to reason using emotions is the ability to harness emotions to help us to think and solve problems. Emotionally intelligent people know how to make the most of their emotions in any situation.

Understanding emotions is being able to understand emotion language and the variations between emotions, and how emotions can change with time.

Managing emotions is the ability to control and change emotions in both ourselves and in others. Those who communicate with charisma are often very skilled in this area.

6

Max Weber and charismatic authority

I believe in benevolent dictatorship provided I am the dictator.

Richard Branson

We can't really talk about what we understand by charisma and what it means to others without mentioning Max Weber and charismatic authority.

Max Weber (1864–1920) was a German sociologist and political economist who is now regarded as one of the founders of modern sociology.

He proposed that there were three different types of authority: charismatic authority, traditional authority and rational-legal authority.

Weber defined charismatic authority as: '… resting on devotion to the exceptional sanctity, heroism or exemplary character of an individual person, and of the normative patterns or order revealed or ordained by him.'

He described charisma as: 'A certain quality of an individual personality, by virtue of which he is set apart from ordinary men and treated as endowed with supernatural, superhuman, or at least specifically exceptional powers or qualities. These are such as are not accessible to the ordinary person, but are regarded as of divine origin or as exemplary, and on the basis of them the individual concerned is treated as a leader.'

Charismatic authority is: '… power legitimized on the basis of a leader's exceptional personal qualities or the demonstration of extraordinary insight and accomplishment, which inspire loyalty and obedience from followers.'

For Weber, charisma was directly related to leadership and authority, especially for leaders in a religious context or dictatorial political sense.

7

Developing your own charisma

Why join the navy if you can be a pirate?

Steve Jobs

We need to take a good look at ourselves to be able to develop our own charisma – this is the only way we can progress. There is not a person living who could not improve himself or herself as a communicator and develop their personal appeal.

We believe that Story, Status and Focus (or SSF) are the keys to our success in this area.

As we explore SSF you must check your present self and how you communicate at the moment; then look for the adjustments you need to make to improve. You'll need to change how you think about yourself. You'll need to change how your think about others. And you'll need to think about how you communicate. If you do so, you'll find that the improvements and adjustments will certainly be there.

Charisma is definitely something that we all have and it is something that we can all develop further and more deeply. We are not saying that it is possible or even desirable to build and develop some sort of magical persona that people can't help but gravitate towards. But it is possible for everyone to develop their own personal brand and make it accessible and attractive to others. Many of us don't like to look at ourselves in any detail, but this is what has to happen to cultivate a more appealing, more attractive persona and communicate with charisma. We need to understand that to develop our own personal charisma we must inspect our image, physically, vocally and emotionally and, if necessary, make changes.

We have all seen actors portray charismatic figures. That doesn't necessarily mean that the actors themselves are hugely charismatic. What it does mean is that they are able to play 'charisma' and do justice to the part they are acting. If that is the case then surely we can do the same – not play parts but change the way we are perceived. We are not suggesting that you try to be someone you are not, but if you recognize the qualities in 'the greats' that make them charismatic then you can develop the same qualities in yourself.

SSF is a powerful formula that will help you to start to feel differently about yourself as a communicator and a performer. It will help you understand your personal brand, your style, your story. It will make you more aware of the importance of storytelling as a mode of communication and the impact it has on our lives. It will help you recognize the value of other people's stories.

It will introduce you to status – the very foundation of charismatic communication. You will be challenged on your physical status. You will be made aware of your vocal status. And chances are that you are not at the moment producing anything like the vocal sound you are capable of. This real vocal status is key to developing your real persona. You will be asked to think and consider emotional status. And come to understand how important it is to the success of great leaders and how it can change our lives for the better.

The secrets of focus will be revealed to you. You will learn that by varying the degrees of your focus and concentration, you will learn to manage the focus of those around you. Be encouraged by American TV personality Conan O'Brien: 'Nobody in life gets exactly what they thought they were going to get, but if you work really hard and you're kind, amazing things will happen.'

Everyone's personal brand of charisma will be different. What they will all have in common are the reactions and feelings they evoke in other people. Charismatic people stir our emotions and generally make us feel good. Charismatic people seem to be able to connect effortlessly with those around them. Charismatic people inspire and motivate. Charismatic people appear open and accessible. We want to be all these things and we can be!

Truly charismatic communicators, whether they know it or not, employ all the benefits of SSF. Only a deep understanding of how SSF can help us to develop our own charisma will be sufficient to really make a difference to our personal growth.

At The Speechworks we have worked with many people from a wide variety of sectors of the community on SSF. We can confidently say that once you have an understanding of the value of employing SSF to your everyday communication, you will be tapping into and increasing your charisma, and you will enjoy a happier and more successful life. Your anxieties will decrease and your confidence will rise. When confidence increases so does competence, and the better you get at what you do the more confident you feel about yourself – on the confidence/competence scale one feeds the other.

To get the most from this book, pay special attention to how Story, Status and Focus impacts on everything we do socially, domestically and in our working lives. Knowing that you are having a positive effect on others and sometimes changing their lives for the better will make you feel good and enrich your life.

The only reason we communicate with people is to have an effect on them; so if we learn to communicate with charisma we ensure that the effect will be the one that we want.

Charisma – a personal view by the Reverend Ruth Scott

Reverend Ruth Scott is an Anglican priest, writer and broadcaster. She was ordained in 1994 as one of Britain's first female priests. She has been a regular presenter of 'Pause for Thought' on BBC Radio 2's 'Wake up to Wogan' and is involved in conflict transformation work and interfaith dialogue. Here she shares her insight with us on what 'charisma' means to her personally. There seems to us a great deal of synergy between her views on what makes for charisma and ours on communicating with charisma.

If you've ever tried to get hold of fine dry sand in your hands, you will know how easily it slips through your fingers the more you try to grasp it. I wonder if the same might be true as I try to get to grips with the nature of charisma. The sociologist and political economist, Max Weber (see Chapter 6), who explored the concept of charisma in some depth, came up with a clear, but in my view, inadequate definition. My starting point will be his definition and why I think it is limited, even misleading. I don't expect to replace it with a better version, but in the process I will articulate some of the characteristics I've observed in people I perceive to be charismatic.

Weber defined charisma as, 'a certain quality of an individual personality, by virtue of which he is set apart from ordinary men and treated as endowed with supernatural, superhuman, or at least specifically exceptional powers or qualities. These are such as are not accessible to the ordinary person, but are regarded as of divine origin or as exemplary, and on the basis of them the individual concerned is treated as a leader...' How the quality in question would be ultimately judged from an ethical, aesthetic, or other such point of view is naturally indifferent for the purpose of definition.

Taking Weber's words on face value it is important to note that charisma is not the same thing as 'goodness', although I suspect the initial reaction of most of us would be to think of it in positive terms. It isn't comfortable to acknowledge that people like Hitler, for example, were charismatic. History shows how millions of Germans hailed Hitler as the saviour of their nation and many carried out acts of heartbreaking inhumanity in support of him. Supporters who met him on a one-to-one basis spoke of the magnetism of his personality. I think it is possible to argue that the power Hitler clearly exerted over his followers was not authentically charismatic because his outlook and purpose lacked many of the characteristics that can be attributed to 'good' charismatic leaders such as Jesus Christ.

Why does one person's charisma find expression through creatively humane words and actions, and another's become channelled through inhumanely corrupt practices? One reason is to do with the relationship between power and love. The twentieth-century theologian and philosopher, Paul Tillich, defined love as 'the drive towards the unity of the separated', and power as 'the drive of everything living to realize itself, with increasing intensity and extensity.' Both these drives have creative and corrupt expressions. They become degenerative when they exist independently of one another. As Martin Luther King, who studied Tillich's ideas for his doctorate, wrote: 'Power without love is reckless and abusive, and love without power is sentimental and anaemic.'

Both Jesus Christ and Martin Luther King are positive charismatic role models for me but to some extent that judgement is subjective. In their own time other people clearly felt very differently. As we see with Hitler, having mass support doesn't necessarily signify a person is right, and many men and women of the past who today are generally regarded as 'good' people were initially lone voices 'crying in the wilderness'. With this in mind I suggest that to speak of someone as being 'charismatic' says as much, if not more, about the perceptions and psyche of the one speaking as it does about the one described as charismatic.

As I think about the men and women I would describe as charismatic I'm conscious that, without exception, they would be uncomfortable about being labelled in this way. Charisma, their own or anyone else's, would be of no interest to them at all. Such charismatic personalities quickly jump off the pedestal that others put them on. As a hero of mine, a highly controversial, and internationally known and loved leader, once said to a fan who was exalting his profoundly insightful books and his humane work, 'I'm as fucked up as the next person.' This friend, I'll call him Peter, would certainly laugh at the idea he was, in Weber's terms 'endowed with supernatural, superhuman, or at least specifically exceptional powers or qualities.'

Peter, like all the other people I would describe as being charismatic, is under no illusions about his flaws and failings. He accepts himself as he is, warts and all, and tries to live and work honestly and compassionately with that reality. He is very self-aware. In this sense he and Hitler are diametrically opposed. Hitler had delusions of grandeur and was in the right place at the right time in the right circumstances to play that role for a people desperate to stand tall again after years of humiliation. He accepted their projections, and believed them. To define someone as having charisma, is another way of saying that they have made a significant connection with the mind *and* heart of the one who defines them as charismatic. Whether this is a positive or negative connection depends upon the nature and needs of the people connected, as I've already illustrated in relation to Hitler.

Does charisma that inspires and builds people up positively depend upon the charismatic leader being 'good'? 'Good' is another relative word. For some people Hitler was a good leader. For others he was a psychologically sick tyrant. For some people Nelson Mandela was an inspirational human being and leader. For others he was a thorn in the flesh, a terrorist. Both captured the spirit of their time and place – the zeitgeist. It was their moment and they lived it. The question is, who did they live it for? For themselves, for others, or for both?

Here I think is a characteristic that distinguishes between a truly charismatic person, and one who draws the crowds but lacks the depth and understanding of his own humanity to be an authentic charismatic. The former does not consider him/herself to be at the centre of their own universe. Their personal needs are not the priority. There are values they have which go beyond selfish considerations. While not being self-abusive they are prepared to make decisions and take action for a cause they believe in that will demand sacrifice on their part.

Peter's self-awareness is not to be confused with being self-obsessed or self-centred. He is a man of integrity and honesty who has tried to learn from the mistakes he has made. His deep humanity and compassion for others arises from the fact that he is well aware of his own 'fucked-up-ness', just as he recognizes and seeks to value and use his gifts.

Charismatic qualities described by Weber as superhuman, supernatural or specifically exceptional are actually rooted in our humanity and are within the capacity of all human beings. In the case of charismatic people like Peter, their specialness is not primarily to do with being good, but to do with being aware of the complexity of their nature and using that understanding to inform the way they respond to wider human experience. Charismatic people are not focused on themselves, but on other people and situations in the world around them. They do not do what they do for self-aggrandizement. They do not deny their abilities but they sit lightly to them, and move beyond them to using them creatively.

We speak about charismatic people having 'presence'. It's what draws others to them. I want to suggest this 'presence' exists because the person is fully present in the moment. Most of us go through the motions of living in the present while being distracted by thoughts and emotions about what's happened in the past or may happen in the future. I think it is those moments when we are 'in' the present moment, being fully alive that we are able to be what others describe as charismatic. In such moments we are 'at home' with ourselves, in all our beauty and brokenness, doing and being what we love doing and being. Perhaps that's why performers can hold an audience spellbound, but come off stage to lives that are a disaster. The at-one-ment they know on stage is not their reality in the rest of their experience.

The task is not to be charismatic, but to be more fully human and alive, inclusive and adventurous, self-aware and self-possessed, as opposed to selfish and self-obsessed. Openness to life in all its many shades is critical. As are curiosity and imagination. Truly charismatic people are not those who think they have all the answers, but are the ones prepared to ask the questions, the next one and the next one and the next one…

Truly charismatic people will not care about being charismatic. They're too busy living to bother about such things. I suspect that when we try simply to live as half-decent human beings saying 'yes' to life, we will quite unconsciously become 'charismatic' in the eyes of others.

Part

02

Introducing Story, Status and Focus – the keys to communicating with charisma

Before beginning, plan carefully.

Cicero

Broadly speaking, the short words are the best, and the old words best of all.

Winston Churchill

8

Story

There have been great societies that did not use the wheel,
but there have been no societies that did not tell stories.

Ursula K. Le Guin

Whatever the message we are trying to communicate
to our audience, getting the story right is absolutely
crucial. Storytelling is our fundamental mode of communication. As humans, we've been telling stories since
time immemorial. We start telling stories from the
moment we learn to speak. We tell stories because it's
the best way of getting people to understand information. Because telling stories is what makes our messages
accessible and memorable, it is crucial that we get the
story right. The most brilliant delivery in the world
will not save badly constructed material. Paying great
attention to the construction of our stories, creating a

fluid journey for our audience and bringing the story to life are all essential aspects of good storytelling.

No matter what the situation – it is important to have a *good* story. Many people in the business world may think 'I have to convey serious pieces of information when I give presentations – there's no room for fooling around telling stories!'

But they're wrong. As part of our role with The Speechworks, we coach and train many senior directors of large corporate organizations in acting and writing skills. More often than not these directors are very quick to tell us how dull and dry their material is, and how the content of their presentation could never be engaging or exciting. This is not a good starting point for anyone who wishes to develop his or her charisma. We too are always very quick to tell them that this is just their perception. Often their assumption that the message is not interesting is the root of the problem with a presentation or speech. Whatever the material, there is always a story there waiting to get out – with a beginning, a middle and an end.

Most of our daily communications have the 'beginnings, middles and ends' that all good stories consist of. So making sure that our speeches, presentations and more formal addresses have the same story structure is vital.

When we listen to great communicators speak there can be no doubt that they have given special attention to assembling their speech and telling their story. Their stories are alive with enthusiasm and spontaneity. They pick us up, take us on a journey – they make us hang on every word.

9

Status

At a round table there is no dispute about place.

Italian proverb

Charismatic communicators have delivery styles we find warm and inviting. We feel at ease with them and personally addressed by them. They seem accessible and strong. This is because they adopt exactly the right level of status.

If you look up 'status' in the dictionary it will tell you that it comes from Latin, and meanings include 'standing' and 'posture'. This may indicate that it is something physical. Yes, it is physical but it is also mental, vocal and emotional.

Status is how we perceive people and how people perceive us. Status can, of course, be determined by hierarchy and positions of seniority but that's not what status is really all about. Status is about how we perceive people no matter what their position. It enables us to make decisions about how to react to people. When we meet someone for the first time we subconsciously ask ourselves three questions:

1 What sex is that person?
2 How old are they?
3 What is their status?

Actors study status when training and rehearsing. It is important that actors understand the extremes of status to portray the character they are playing effectively and how status will affect that character's level of charisma. People in business or public life do not have the luxury of experimenting with status in the way that actors do. They have to get it right the first time.

The status scale of 1 to 10

Finding the right level of status to be effective in our business, public or personal lives is the central pillar of communicating with charisma. On a status scale of 1 to 10, 1 isn't the worst and 10 certainly isn't the best. We need to be hitting the middle status ground of 5 to 7 every time. We don't want to appear aloof or arrogant (10) nor do we want to apologize timidly for ourselves (1).

Bill Clinton is one person who seems to get his status level right every time. When making a speech, when being interviewed, even when out in public. After the horrors of 9/11 when George Bush looked like a rabbit caught in the headlights, Clinton was walking the streets hugging people. The public were literally throwing themselves into his arms! Why? Because he was open, warm, receptive and strong. Which was exactly what the people needed at that time. He had charisma.

It is very difficult to argue with, or take offence at, the middle ground – an open and neutral status. It is the closest we are ever likely to get to being and acting the same with everyone we meet. When we at The Speechworks first started working with business clients on status we asked a clinical psychologist if it was possible for someone to be the same with everyone. The psychologist thought for a moment and replied, 'Yes, but they would probably have to be sectioned.' So the next time you hear someone say, 'Oh, I'm the same with everyone – king, queen, peasant, pauper. What you see is what you get with me', run a mile because they are clearly raving mad!

The right level

Getting the level of status right isn't just applicable to those who have to stand and speak. It is just as important in every other area of our working lives. When coaching a senior director of a FTSE 100 company recently, we soon discovered that it wasn't just his presentation style that his company training department wanted us to look at. They also wanted us to change his behaviour in the workplace. This particular individual was tall and physically quite imposing. He also, rather proudly, assumed a very high level of status vocally, mentally and emotionally. He almost seemed to enjoy stomping around like Godzilla and bawling at people.

A challenging brief but we came up with a strategy that satisfied both agendas. He was very eager to learn about charisma and how it could improve his presentation skills. So our plan was to work heavily on status. In order to seamlessly adopt the open, warm, receptive level of status required to be an effective presenter, we insisted that this level be maintained at all times. We asked him to check his level of status with every piece of communication he had in his working day. The result was a behavioural transformation with his colleagues. He found that hitting the right level of status changed how he behaved and also improved how he was perceived by others.

By hitting that 5–7 level of status, great communicators make themselves totally accessible to their audiences. Anything lower would result in a reduction of audience respect and so close him off. Anything higher would run the risk of making an audience feel that they were being spoken down to. The chapters in this book on status will give a great insight into the value and importance of achieving that charisma level of status.

10

Focus

Act the part and you will become the part.

William James

The third element of charisma is focus, the icing on the cake. The truly great communicators have focus in spades. And whether they know it or not, they have a Russian theatre director and acting innovator, born in 1863, to thank for it.

Konstantin Sergeyevich Stanislavski was the co-founder of the Moscow Art Theatre, the founder of the first acting system – Stanislavski's System – and a great exponent of the naturalist school of thought. He was also the inspiration behind Lee Strasberg's 'Method' School of Acting in New York City to which many acting greats subscribe, including Robert

De Niro, Dustin Hoffman, Dame Judi Dench and Anthony Hopkins to name just a few.

Stanislavski's circles of concentration

Stanislavski's circles of concentration, or attention, are the professional actor's fundamental source of on-stage focus. They are an unbelievably powerful tool that should not be restricted to the world of film and theatre. Stanislavski once said: 'If the ability to receive the creative mood in its full measure is given to genius by nature, then perhaps ordinary people may reach a like state after a great deal of hard work with themselves – not in its full measure, but at least in part.'

Whether or not charismatic communicators have acquired this creative focus naturally, it is without doubt one of the most powerful weapons in the armoury. When they speak we get a real sense that they are sharing something of themselves with us. This is partially due to the level of status they adopt, but also because of the ability to manage the focus of their performance and the focus of the audience. Some would say it's a certain '*Je ne sais quoi*', others might say that it's 'star quality' but we know that it is in fact, focus.

The ability to use and harness focus turns a competent address into a truly compelling performance. Would an audience prefer to sit through an adequately delivered address or be highly entertained? Great performances have a huge impact on us, which is why much emphasis must be placed on the subject of focus and concentration. Take two very different performers in two different situations with two very different subject matters. Martin Luther King with his 'I had a dream' speech made in Washington DC in 1963, and Robert De Niro playing the lonely, deranged Vietnam veteran in *Taxi Driver*. Both expertly manage our focus with the crafted distribution of their own focus and technique.

Shakespeare said: 'All the world's a stage' and he wasn't wrong. As coaches in presentation and communication skills, we at The Speechworks have gained enormous pleasure from introducing the world of commerce and public life to the theories and practices of theatre and screen. There is increasing commonality between people in business, public figures, politicians and entertainers. Today, more than ever, it's all about performance. And performance is all about focus. *Charisma* explains Stanislavski's Circles of Concentration and how you can learn and apply them with maximum effect.

Let's take a look in more detail at how SSF will help develop our charisma.

Part

03

Communicating with charisma – **Story**, Status, Focus

Directing a film was something I was yearning to do. I always wanted to see if I had the capacity to be a good storyteller.

Kevin Spacey

Whatever words we utter should be chosen with care for people will hear them and be influenced by them for good or ill.

Buddha

11

Stories – our basic mode of communication

One of the three keys to unlocking the secret of communicating with charisma is to understand the importance of story in how we communicate. But what do we mean by a story? There are many dictionary definitions of story. But let's look at this one.

A piece of narrative, tale of any length, told or printed in prose or verse, based on either true or fictitious events, legend, myth, anecdote, designed to interest, amuse, or instruct the hearer or reader.

A natural feel for narrative, which comes from the Latin, *narrare* – to recount – is crucial if we are to learn from the examples of great charismatic communicators.

Why do we tell stories?

Storytelling is our basic language. We have been telling stories since time began. It's our most natural and elemental form of communication. It has been with us since the beginning. It is how we most easily convey our thoughts, feelings and ideas. It's at the very heart of the human condition.

Imagine our ancestors way back in the dawn of time returning from a hunt. They would have stories to tell of the massive mammoth that somehow mysteriously got away. They would have stories of how they were almost killed by a fierce and savage, sabre-toothed tiger. They would have stories of bravery, success and happiness when they came home triumphant from the heroes' hunt. They would also tell tales of deep disappointment, fear and death. Stories with a happy ending or stories with an unhappy ending – we humans are still telling those elemental stories today.

It is interesting looking back to the stories and communication skills of primitive man to think that cave paintings were actually drawn to help illustrate the stories that were being told. The earliest known example of a PowerPoint presentation perhaps?

Passing on information and knowledge

The oral tradition of storytelling allowed humans to pass on information and knowledge from group to group and from generation to generation. Way back when, stories explained the many events that were beyond our control – droughts, floods, storms, plagues, thunder. These works of nature must have been both frightening and awe-inspiring to our ancestor. So by telling stories they learned to come to terms with these events. They also learned to prepare the next generation to be aware of them – by telling the same stories.

Stories about gods, goddesses, heroes and heroines helped people develop and protect a shared belief system, which would bind them closer together, while stories with a moral element were ways of helping the development of customs and behavioural codes.

Almost every culture in the world has a tradition of storytelling. It is interesting to note that the storytellers were often the elders of the community. They told their stories to pass on valuable information and wisdom, ensuring that it would not be lost. Elder storytellers were always highly respected members of their society. People who could tell a great tale of heroic deeds or amazing escape from disaster were highly regarded and valued by their kin.

The truly great communicators know that story is just as powerful and effective a force now as it always has been. Indeed it is probably more powerful today than ever before. In this digital, globally connected age, story as a form of communication is more pervasive than at any time in history. We are surrounded by stories – news stories on TV, in the press and on the internet. Soap opera stories, stories in film, theatre and books. Gossip stories about celebrities that start on the street and are spread around the world on the web. Stories are universal – all of us respond to a story.

12

Getting the story right

I cannot tell how the truth may be; I say the tale as it was said to me.

Walter Scott

Types of story

As we all know, there are many types and genre of story from parable, myth, legend and fairy tales to love stories, ghost stories, horror stories and urban legend.

In his fascinating and monumental book *The Seven Basic Plots: Why We Tell Stories*, Christopher Booker puts forward the idea that there are in fact only seven different story types. They are:

- Overcoming the Monster
- Rags to Riches
- The Quest
- Voyage and Return
- Comedy
- Tragedy
- Rebirth.

For any reader whom wants to know more about story and why humans tell them, we strongly recommend the book. Booker asserts that every story told, whether it be in a book, in a film, on TV, at the theatre or even the opera, will fit one of these seven basic plots or sometimes a combination of them.

In Overcoming the Monster, the hero, heroes or heroine of the story is faced with a terrifying, powerful monster that must be confronted and defeated. This often happens in a climactic fight to the death. This plot type is found in countless stories including *Beowulf*, the *Epic of Gilgamesh*, *Jaws* and *Dracula*.

In Rags to Riches, the story revolves around a humble, insignificant or unexceptional character whose hidden, amazing talents or gifts are revealed to the world. The character is finally recognized for being what they really are. And everyone lives happily every after. This plot can be seen in *Cinderella*, the Superman stories, *The Ugly Duckling* and *Pygmalion*.

In The Quest, the story is told of a hero, often with comrades, who embarks on a perilous journey in pursuit of priceless treasure or a highly sought-after prize. The journey is always dangerous. They must fight to overcome evil and secure the prize at the end of the quest. This plot is seen in so many stories from the *Odyssey* and the *Aeneid* to *Raiders of the Lost Ark* and *Lord of the Rings*.

In Voyage and Return, the story involves our hero moving from one world or environment into another that is cut off the former. After thrilling and often dangerous experiences the character escapes back to the world that they left. This plot is seen in *Alice in Wonderland*, *Avatar*, *Back to the Future*, and *The Lion, the Witch and the Wardrobe*.

In Comedy, the story is one of confusion and misunderstanding reigning between the protagonists. The situation becomes evermore chaotic, but then to everyone's relief, everything is resolved for a happy ending. This plot type is seen in *All's Well That Ends Well*, *Arms and the Man* and *Some Like It Hot*.

In Tragedy, the story plot shows someone who, through a flaw in their character, is led to disaster by a series of actions. This plot type can be seen in *King Lear*, *Macbeth* and *Oedipus the King*.

Finally in Rebirth, a hero is faced with a sense of increasing threat by an approaching dark force. The force takes control and seems to have triumphed. But a reversal of power takes place and the hero is saved and redeemed. This plot type can be seen in *A Christmas Carol*, *Beauty and the Beast*, *It's a Wonderful Life* and *Peer Gynt*.

When the story being told fits in with one of these basic plot types it perhaps resonates with the audience because they recognize and understand the plot shape. And when the story plot doesn't meet expectations the audience is left feeling dissatisfied – aware that something is not quite right.

Five essentials of a good story

There is one thing that all these forms of story and plot type have in common. And that's structure. By structure we mean the way the story is constructed. These stories always have a beginning, middle and an end. This three-part structure is just one of the five essential components of story that the great communicators seem to have mastery of. They are:

1 Structure
2 Journey
3 Fluidity
4 Brevity
5 Life.

Let us take a closer look at them.

1 Structure

The importance of structure in a story cannot be emphasized too much. Just as we recognize and admire the structure of a beautiful building that has been conceived and designed by a talented architect, so we recognize and admire the structure of a well-crafted story.

We may do this subconsciously. We may not know that we are doing it. But the structure of a story impacts on us enormously. Remember a time when you left the cinema having seen a great movie which told a great story that really resonated with you? You couldn't help but feel inspired, moved and touched by what you'd just seen – the tale you'd been told.

Now remember those times when you'd seen a movie that didn't quite connect with you, didn't move you, didn't make you feel. Chances are it was because the structure of the film just didn't work – it was the story that didn't satisfy. You left the cinema feeling disappointed and let down.

Most stage plays have three acts. Most great movies can be seen as three-act stories. Three seems to be a magic number. And the great communicators know this. Whether they're making a speech or talking one-to-one, they know to keep to their message in the three-act form.

The three-act structure allows for a dramatically satisfying three-fold pattern of events:

Act 1) The set-up

Act 2) The confrontation

Act 3) The resolution.

Now in a Hollywood movie this could be:

1 A cop finds his best friend brutally murdered and vows to find the killer.

2 He sets off on his quest to avenge his friend's death.

3 He finds the killer and brings him to justice. END

This three-act structure works equally well for a business leader explaining to his colleagues that:

1 The company's future is being threatened by economic conditions.

2 The leader and team have to change the way they operate or face bankruptcy.

3 The leader and team must find the solution and make it a reality. END

When the great communicators connect with their audience they ensure that the message has this three-act structure, with which their audience is both familiar and comfortable.

2 Journey

When we were children and we heard those magical words 'once upon a time' we knew we were off on a wonderful journey to encounter all sorts of exciting adventures along the way. Why can't speeches and presentations be like that? Well, they can be and they should be! We do it for children so why can't adults have the same exciting adventures along the way?

The great communicators know how important it is to create the feeling of travel in their speeches and presentations because it helps make their message memorable. Like Christopher Booker's story types of Voyage and Return and The Quest, we too need to take our audiences on a journey so, just like when they were children, they will experience a great sense of movement from our story, allowing us to carry them to exactly where we want them to be.

3 Fluidity

Great stories flow seamlessly. The great communicators know that it's the job of the storyteller to take any difficulty out of following the story. Audiences deserve to be put in a position of comfort and ease in order to take on board what they are being told. This will never happen if they have to work hard to see how the story hangs together. The great communicators know how to find the links and the connecting thought processes to tell their story with ease.

This means that their audience is swept along effortlessly on the story's journey. Being carried along by well-crafted material can be a delightful experience.

4 Brevity

Edit, edit and edit again!

We all have difficulty being concise in our communications sometimes. But great communicators show that it's vital to be as concise and succinct as possible. When you are concise in what you say, clarity often follows.

What they do is edit, cut, streamline and trim their material down to a level where it's as succinct, clear and memorable as possible.

Do the five-minute test. Say to yourself 'If I had to tell this story in five minutes, what would I throw out? What is not essential to this tale?' Once you have the message down to the bare bones, then maybe you can look at putting a little more flesh on them to make the story more interesting.

This isn't easy.

As Mark Twain is often wrongly attributed as having said: 'I didn't have time to write a short letter, so I wrote a long one instead.' As Woodrow Wilson did say: 'If I am to speak ten minutes, I need a week for preparation; if fifteen minutes, three days; if half an hour, two days; if an hour, I am ready now.'

It takes discipline and ruthlessness to edit, edit, edit, but every time we do it, the end result is better, more forceful material.

5 Life

Bring it to life.

Part of the power of story and its appeal is that we were told stories at a very early age. As children we loved stories of princes and princesses, of magical lands. We were scared by stories of wicked witches. We were enchanted by stories of mythical beasts.

We also love telling children stories ourselves. And when we tell children stories do we always tell them in the same monotonous, flat voice? No of course we don't. We bring them to life with the range of our voice. We use different voices for the Goody and the Baddy. We cackle like witches or wizards for dramatic effect. We bring the story to life.

When we tell jokes and humorous stories to friends we do exactly the same thing. We use our voice to make the story live. We use our hands, arms and facial expressions to emphasize particular aspects of the story. We become performers. And that's exactly what the great communicators do when they tell their stories to any audience – big or small. They bring the story to life through performance.

The sure-fire way to generate interest from an audience and have the desired effect on them is to show the audience enthusiasm, both for them and for the story, because enthusiasm, as we all know, is infectious. The great communicators never forget that every single piece of communication can be a story.

13

The story of me

Truly charismatic people are not those who think they have all the answers, but are the ones prepared to ask the questions.

The Reverend Ruth Scott

One of the stories that all great communicators tell, and tell well, is their own personal story. In the speech extracts we selected for the end of this book there are many examples of the great communicators telling aspects of their own story – often as part of another story.

So if we want to learn from the greats we need to be able to tell our own personal story too. And to tell our own story it's essential that we know our story, our pull, our draw, our brand.

To be great communicators we must be comfortable with that story and able to tell it well, so it's important that we are self-aware. We need to be able to examine who we are. We must acknowledge our strengths and identify the areas in which we are weak.

This personal audit when finding our own story is not self-obsessive, it is essential to our development as communicators. We have to ask the questions. This kind of questioning helps us find out what we like and don't like about ourselves and gives us the opportunity to make some changes. It will not change who we are but it will allow us to make adjustments. There are many different roles within all of us and many parts to play – we just haven't found them all yet.

Self-examination and adjustments to our persona will not change who we are but they can change, for the better, how we are perceived and how we communicate.

Michael Jackson said: 'I'm starting with the man in the mirror – I'm asking him to change his ways.' If we decide that we want to re-brand ourselves in this way it will not destroy our core character, but it may well help to define our charisma. The chapters in this book on status and focus will help with this reflective process.

Once we have discovered our story and are comfortable with it, all sorts of benefits ensue. We are able to think in a more positive way and have greater clarity of thought. We are able to understand and appreciate the make-up of other people's characters and interact with them in a more effective manner. We feel generally better about ourselves and more confident. Your personal story is important – it is there to support you and underpin your confidence.

14

Listening – tell us another one

A bore is someone who talks about themselves when you want to talk about yourself.

Anon

Charismatic communicators are genuinely interested in other people's stories. And we need to be so, too. Listening to another person's story provides us with information about that person which may be of great worth to us – information after all is power. But there's a much bigger benefit of learning to listen well. Showing interest in what someone else is saying can play a major roll in increasing our charismatic appeal. Of course, people enjoy talking about themselves but they also like people who listen. If they are listened to properly, in an active way, they will be drawn to the listener.

When actors train they study and master many different types of listening. Here are five types of listening that we believe everyone should be aware of if they are to improve their communication skills. The great communicators are always masters of the last type of listening.

Arrogant listening

We've all been a victim of this and we might have been guilty of it ourselves too. The sort who greets what you have to say with the 'Yeah, yeah, yeah … me too … been there, done that, got the T-shirt … you're not telling me anything I don't know already …' attitude. What a turn off!

Distracted listening

Distracted, passive or detached listening is a style of listening that we have all experienced. It's when the person you are talking to is there in body but not in mind. They seem totally disengaged from what you are saying and distracted by anything other than what you are saying to them. It's horrible – they give the impression that they are not interested in you and that they would clearly like either to be somewhere else or be talking to someone else.

Interrupted listening

This one's a killer – or you certainly wish to kill as a result of it! Interrupted listening is practised by people who want to talk about something else, and look for opportunities to butt in and change the direction of what you are saying. Or even worse, have already decided how your thought and sentence should end, so say it for you. They are not really listening at all and are incapable of proper communication.

Aggressive listening

This can be really irritating. The aggressive listener is *so* determined to show you that they *are* listening, often through OTT body language and facial expressions, that they are not actually hearing a single word you say. They make you want to scream, 'Don't show me you're listening – just listen for goodness' sake!' This type of listening isn't just false, it totally devalues you as a person and what you have to say. There's also another form of this, the argumentative listener – they only listen so that they can disagree with you. Both of these types should be avoided at all costs.

Active listening

First coined by the psychologist Thomas Gordon, this is real and genuine listening. It's effective listening. This is where we all need to be when we communicate. CNN's Larry King said, 'I remind myself every morning: Nothing I *say* this day will teach me anything. So if I'm going to learn, I must do it by listening.'

If we take a genuine interest in what another person has to say and allow our comments and our non-verbal leakage to flow as a natural result of what we are hearing – we will be listening actively. It demonstrates clearly that we care about 'who' the person is and 'what they have to say'. It shows that we respect them and find what they have to say interesting.

It shows that we want to hear their story! People who communicate with charisma are active listeners.

Let Ernest Hemingway have the last word: 'When people talk, listen completely. Most people never listen.'

15

Rhetoric in communicating with charisma

I use emotion for the many and reserve reason for the few.
Adolf Hitler

The great communicators and those who communicate with charisma are often, if not always, very talented orators. They understand the power of rhetoric.

Rhetoric, the art of using language to communicate effectively and persuasively, was highly regarded by the ancient Greeks. And because the ancient Greeks valued the public's participation in the political forum, rhetoric became a useful tool for influencing politics. Because of this, rhetoric is generally associated with its political origins and speechmaking. But rhetoric can be equally useful in how we tell our stories in a multitude of ways.

So who of us can benefit from knowing a little about rhetoric? Anyone with a story to tell. And that's a story in our business lives or personal lives. An informal talk told to a small group of colleagues, an important presentation or a keynote speech; they'd all become better stories with the intelligent use of rhetoric.

Rhetoric is based on three appeals or methods of persuasion, which can be used to support an argument or make a point. Aristotle termed these appeals ethos, logos, and pathos.

Ethos is the appeal to the authority, the honesty and the standing of the speaker in the eyes of whomever they are talking to. It's about gaining respect and trust.

Logos is the logical appeal and method of persuasion. Those points or parts of our stories, which appeal to the logical, rational side of our audience. Figures, statistics, numbers and facts statistics are all part of logos.

Pathos is the appeal to the emotions. It's the type of persuasion we use when we want to change how people feel; to get them to think differently about something, to change their opinions or change the way they act.

Great communicators use just the right combination of ethos, logos and pathos.

Aristotle described rhetoric as: 'The faculty of discovering in any particular case all of the available means of persuasion.' In the words of Plato: 'Rhetoric is the art of ruling the minds of men.' while Cicero believed that: 'Nothing is so unbelievable that oratory cannot make it acceptable.'

And from the dark side of charisma, in the words of Hitler: 'The broad masses of a population are more amenable to the appeal of rhetoric than to any other force.'

Rhetoric is invaluable in bringing our stories to life, making them memorable and giving them the impact we desire. To get what the greats have got and to communicate your stories with charisma, it helps to be aware of these simple techniques of rhetoric.

Alliteration

The repetition of the same sound at the beginning of several words in a sequence. It is used for stressing an important point or for making something more memorable. Examples are:

Veni, vidi, vici.

Julius Caesar

Let us go forth to lead the land we love.

John F. Kennedy

And our nation itself is testimony to the love our veterans have had for it and for us. All for which America stands is safe today because brave men and women have been ready to face the fire at freedom's front.

Ronald Reagan

Anadiplosis

The repetition of the last word of the preceding clause. The word ending a sentence or clause is used again to begin the next sentence or clause. Examples are:

They call for you: the general who became a slave; the slave who became a gladiator; the gladiator who defied an emperor.

Commodus in the film *Gladiator*

The land of my fathers. My fathers can have it.

Dylan Thomas

Anaphora

The repetition of a word or phrase at the beginning of successive sentences, phrases or clauses. It is a powerful way of increasing impact. Examples are:

We shall fight on the beaches,
we shall fight on the landing grounds,
we shall fight in the fields and in the streets …

Winston Churchill

This royal throne of kings, this sceptred isle,
This earth of majesty, this seat of Mars,
This other Eden, demi-paradise,
This fortress built by Nature for herself …

Shakespeare (*Richard II*)

What we need in the United States is not division.
What we need in the United States is not hatred.
What we need in the United States is not violence and lawlessness; but is love and wisdom and compassion toward one another, and a feeling of justice toward those who still suffer within our country whether they be white or whether they be black.

Robert F. Kennedy on the death of Luther King

Antistrophe

The repetition of the same word or phrase at the end of successive clauses. Another powerful way of increasing impact – less used today but very effective when implemented. Examples are:

In 1931, ten years ago, Japan invaded Manchukuo – without warning. In 1935, Italy invaded Ethiopia – without warning. In 1938, Hitler occupied Austria – without warning. In 1939, Hitler invaded Czechoslovakia – without warning. Later in 1939, Hitler invaded Poland – without warning. And now Japan has attacked Malaya and Thailand – and the United States – without warning.

Franklin D. Roosevelt

… and that government of the people, by the people, for the people shall not perish from the earth.

Abraham Lincoln

Antithesis

Setting opposites together to bring out the contrast in meaning. Examples are:

Not that I loved Cæsar less, but that I loved Rome more.

William Shakespeare (*Julius Cæsar*)

We must learn to live together as brothers or perish together as fools.

Martin Luther King

For many are called, but few are chosen.

St Matthew 22:14 (AV)

Aporia

A technique in which the speaker expresses doubt or uncertainty about what to say, think or do. The doubt may be genuine or not. 'Well, what can I say?' is the simplest example.

Asyndeton

Also known as asyndetism. This is when conjunctions between co-ordinate phrases are deliberately left out for dramatic effect. Examples are:

… and that government of the people, by the people, for the people shall not perish from the earth. (This is also alliterative – see above)

Abraham Lincoln

… we shall pay any price, bear any burden, meet any hardship, support any friend, oppose any foe to assure the survival and the success of liberty.

John F. Kennedy

Assonance

The repetition of the same vowel sound to create rhyming or rhythm. It can help emphasis and memorability. Examples are:

How now brown cow

Unknown

The rain in Spain stays mainly in the plain

Film *My Fair Lady*

The gloves didn't fit. If it doesn't fit, you must acquit.

Johnny Cochran, concluding arguments in the O.J. Simpson trial

Cacophony

Juxtaposition of words to produce a harsh or jarring sound, such as:

We want no parlay with you and your grisly gang who work your wicked will.

Winston Churchill

Catachresis

The misapplication of a word, especially in a mixed metaphor or the use of a word in a sense that is very different from its normal sense. A good example is:

'Tis deepest winter in Lord Timon's purse.

Shakespeare (*Timon of Athens*)

Chiasmus

This is when the words in one phrase or clause are reversed in the next. Examples are:

Mankind must put an end to war or war will put an end to mankind.

John F. Kennedy

People the world over have always been more impressed by the power of our example than by the example of our power.

Bill Clinton

The true test is not the speeches the president delivers; it's if the president delivers on the speeches.

Hillary Clinton

Diacope

This is the repetition of the same word or phrase on either side of an intervening word or phrase, for example:

The people everywhere, not just here in Britain, everywhere – they kept faith with Princess Diana.

Tony Blair

Hyperbole

Exaggeration used for emphasis or effect. The philosopher Seneca said that hyperbole 'asserts the incredible in order to arrive at the credible.' Like this:

You were lucky. We lived for three months in a brown paper bag in a septic tank. We used to have to get up at six o'clock in the morning, clean the bag, eat a crust of stale bread, go to work down't mill for 14 hours a day week in, week out. When we got home, our dad would thrash us to sleep with his belt!

From *Monty Python's Flying Circus*

Litotes

An understatement used to describe the expression of an idea by the denial of its opposite – often as a double negative. 'You are not wrong' or 'He's not the most charismatic person I know' are good examples. Here's another:

We made a difference. We made the city stronger, we made the city freer, and we left her in good hands. All in all, not bad, not bad at all.

Ronald Reagan

Metaphor

An implied comparison achieved through the figurative use of words. Among many possible examples are:

An iron curtain has descended across the continent.

Winston Churchill

All the world's a stage,
And all the men and women merely players;
They have their exits and their entrances ...

Shakespeare

No man is an island

John Donne

Paradox

A statement which appears to contradict itself but may be true. An example is:

I have found the paradox, that if you love until it hurts, there can be no more hurt, only more love.

Mother Teresa

Paralipsis

This is a way of emphasizing a point by seeming to pass over it. A pretended or apparent omission which highlights the point by saying in some way that you will not talk about it. Very calculated, this one:

Let us make no judgement on the events of Chappaquiddick, since the facts are not yet all in.

Political opponent of Senator Edward Kennedy

Personification

Giving a personality to an impersonal object or thing. Great communicators use this to bring ideas to life and help an audience relate to concepts or arguments. A well-known example, two perhaps not, but very effective:

England expects every man to do his duty.

Lord Nelson

Art is a jealous mistress and, if a man has a genius for painting, poetry, music, architecture, or philosophy, he makes a bad husband, and an ill provider.

Ralph Waldo Emerson

O beware, my lord, of jealousy!
It is the green-eyed monster which doth mock
The meat it feeds on.

Shakespeare (*Othello*)

Sylepsis

In which one word is used in two different senses:

We must all hang together or assuredly we will all hang separately.

Benjamin Franklin

The rule of three

Great communicators also understand the power of the rule of three – also called triplets or tricolon. It's a very simple and effective technique where they repeat something three times for increased impact. Many likely examples include:

There are three kinds of lies: lies, damned lies, and statistics.

Benjamin Disraeli

May all of you as Americans never forget your heroic origins, never fail to seek divine guidance and never lose your natural, God-given optimism.

Ronald Reagan

Education, Education, Education.

Tony Blair

Emphasis

When writing for the written word we can use exclamation marks to emphasize a point. But for the spoken word there are other, better techniques. Using the natural rhythm of sentences can be very effective if we remember that the end of a sentence has the most impact for the listener and that the beginning of a sentence has the second most impact. The great communicators know instinctively to place the most important points that they're making at the end and at the beginning of their sentences.

Part
04

Communicating with charisma – Story, **Status**, Focus

I've spent my whole life being told I have a face like a horse. You are just what you are, aren't you?

Jeremy Paxman

First, I'm trying to prove to myself that I'm a person. Then maybe I'll convince myself that I'm an actress.

Marilyn Monroe

16

Status and charisma

My old drama coach used to say, 'Don't just do something, stand there.' Gary Cooper wasn't afraid to do nothing.

Clint Eastwood

The kind of status we are talking about has little to do with positions of authority or social standing. Status is about how we perceive people and how we are perceived regardless of position or hierarchy.

Status and self-esteem

Does status have anything to do with self-esteem? Well, perhaps – but self-esteem is really about how we feel about ourselves rather than how we are perceived by others. While we understand that certain overlaps can be found between self-esteem and status the two should not be confused – we can all demonstrate characteristics of low or high status without suffering from low or high self-esteem – there is a big difference. Our charisma is judged by others.

The three questions

Status is about the conscious effect we have on others and the conscious or sub-conscious effect others have on us. We spoke about the three sub-conscious questions we ask ourselves when meeting someone for the first time:

1 What sex is that person?
2 How old are they?
3 What is their status?

We cannot help but ask these questions. The first two questions do, of course, have a bearing on how we react to that person but the question about status will, whether we know it at the time or not, end up being the most important of the three. What is that person's status? What is that person's status compared with mine? Is it higher or lower? Is it similar? What kind of effect are they going to have on me? How should I behave with them? If I had to, how would I play this person? All valid questions and all asked subconsciously.

Self-importance – beware

As we said earlier, status is not about position, importance or even how we view our own importance. A senior business figure we encountered was rather boastful after returning from a first-class cruise on a luxury liner – he said, 'Do you know, the Chief Purser came up to me and said that I was the most important person on the ship!' Surely the Captain would have something to say about that? It is safe to say this kind of delusional twit would have no idea what status is even if he read this book.

The importance of status

Status is probably the most important component when communicating with charisma and is certainly the key topic of this book. We can have the best story ever written and a total mastery of focus, but if we adopt the wrong level of status we will close down our ability to communicate effectively. The effects of low and high self-esteem can be pretty devastating, ranging from self-loathing to suicide of the low, and boastful bullying to hardened criminality in the high. The effects of low and high status are not nearly as dangerous as this but can have an extremely negative impact on our lives nevertheless. It is therefore most important that we get our status levels right.

It is crucial that we understand the extremes of status so that we can hit the most palatable and effective level for our lives. Whether we know it or not we are constantly commenting on the status of others – 'He's really cocky' … 'She's quite timid' … 'She's so abrupt' … 'He wouldn't say boo to a goose' … these remarks are all about how we perceive other people – how we rank their status. When the remarks are less critical and more flattering – 'I've got a lot of time for him' … 'I feel I've known her for ages' … the right level of status is being adopted. We are in charisma territory. Remember that on a scale of 1–10, 5–7 is the channel we need to be in if we are to acquire and project charisma. The major part of communicating successfully is allowing people to communicate with us by making ourselves accessible. Being 'abrupt' or 'cocky' is a turn-off that will make us inaccessible in the same way that being timid will close us down. We're talking about social skills, and these extremes of status will only act as barriers to good communication. Let's stay with the extremes of status and explore the negative effects they have.

Status manipulation

After running a status workshop for an eminent record company during which we focused on the extremes of status and how to be wary of status abuse, we had a call from their Head of Training and Development who had attended the workshop. She had an amusing tale to tell. Only a matter of days after our visit there was a knock on her door. One of her staff wanted a word. Rather than entering the office and sitting opposite her boss, she decided to walk around the desk and crouch down next to her. She cocked her head on one side and looked up at her boss with 'cow eyes'. The boss stood up, pulled the girl to her feet and led her to the office sofa. They sat on the same level as each other and the boss asked the girl what it was she wanted. After a brief conversation the girl's request was denied and she left the room. The Head of Training believed she was being set up as a victim of low status manipulation, and had she not recognized the tactic she may well have granted an unrealistic request.

Low status abuse

Is it possible to fall victim to a low status abuser? Does low status abuse exist? Yes it does, and it's much more subtle and sinister than its high status counterpart. Low status abuse is devious and manipulative. Unlike its brash opposite it can be difficult to detect and even more deadly. Low status abuse does not manifest itself organically; it is cunningly acquired and cynically practised for personal gain. Low status abusers are not prone to unabashed outbursts like their conflicting opponents; they wait patiently for an opportune moment when the victim's guard is down before inflicting their lethal sting.

We have all experienced a low status bashing with words like – 'Oh, you're so clever you – you're brilliant – I wish I could be like you – no really you are – you are brilliant – I could never do anything like that – aren't you clever – isn't she clever everyone?....' Argggggghhh!! Go away!

Deliberate self-deprecation and the bolstering of others are the low status abuser's chief weapons. With carefully chosen words that ruefully run themselves down and wistfully praise others, the low status abuser moves in for the kill. The really skilful low status abuser will achieve their objective without their victim even noticing they've been had.

We've all encountered someone who makes us want to put them down. The kind of person who cringes around us – who is coweringly sweet – who irritates the heck out of us with this self-imposed subjugation – and if we pull this person up or level criticism at them, we're the big bad wolf. We are the ones that everyone will look sideways at for the rest of the day and the low status manipulator has got us again! Watch out – it's subtle but deadly. This kind of low status strategy is not attractive, it is certainly not charismatic, it destroys our ability to communicate properly and is best tackled by canny middle status intervention.

High status abuse

High status behaviour is usually quite blatant and in your face. It is frequently used to intimidate and bully and is often adopted by people who don't actually want to communicate properly in case they might be wrong. People with narcissistic personality disorders often assume a higher level of status because it reinforces their love of themselves and their belief that it is everybody else who is out of step.

In a recent interview, author and actor Stephen Fry was speaking of responsibility when he said – '... duty, obligation, responsibility are all words that I have fought against all my life ... if you feel you are doing something through responsibility – don't do it – but do project how you might feel if you don't do it ... reneging on my word would make me deeply unhappy.'

That kind of sentiment would probably never enter the head of an extremely high status person because they would not care if they let other people down. Even worse, they might wish their behaviour to have a harmful effect on those around them. Some high status owners actually get a perverse pleasure from subjecting others to this kind of status abuse. Let's not forget our purple-rage, furniture-throwing chap at the beginning of the book who actually believed he was justified in tearing strips off people and reducing them to quivering wrecks. This kind of behaviour is the antithesis of good communication. It will have a negative impact on those around him and his company's success. Fear does not equal respect. The only way to counteract behaviour like this is through middle status, 5–7, the charisma channel. If we engage high with high, a long and bloody war of attrition will ensue with no winner. It is difficult to take offence at middle status and its undeniable strength. We should never be afraid of high level status – high status abusers are like animals that smell fear, and pounce!

Marking out the territory

Animalistic behaviour with high status abusers is quite common. One particularly high status individual we coached displayed some typical territorial tendencies. On entering the room for an initial meeting he rearranged every single piece of furniture, including the hat stand and the waste-paper basket, before sitting down. He might as well have peed up every wall! 5–7 will do the trick. At worst, the high status abuser will get frustrated with middle status and at best they will adjust their level of status to communicate in a less arrogant way. Either way the effect will be more positive than negative and definitely more palatable.

Give and take

We should never feel the need to prove our status and we should never claim status, as it will make us look insecure. This is, of course, the classic error of the high status abuser. We should also never try to take status. Saddam Hussein took it and therefore had it to lose. Let's think of a memorable image of Saddam Hussein, one that was shown on TV so often. Saddam on the balcony in his hunting tweeds, chest puffed out, watching the troops parade past, shotgun in hand, firing off the shotgun. It doesn't get much more high status than that. Now let's think of other images; the image of Saddam being pulled out of a hole in the ground, the image of Saddam being photographed in his underpants, the image of someone poking around in his mouth with their fingers. Was he high status then? No sir.

When there is a dramatic change in a person's status it is invariably from high to low, usually resulting in a loss of charismatic appeal. George Shultz, American Secretary of State, said of Margaret Thatcher:

'If I were married to her, I'd be sure to have the dinner ready when she got home!'

Margaret Thatcher was in a high status position as Prime Minister. She was also naturally a fairly high status person who played high status. When the men in grey suits came to visit, however, and she had to leave Number 10, and had to walk to her car in tears, her status had crumbled. This dramatic change in status never seems to happen the other way.

The law of the jungle

Extreme low status can be equally as negative and unproductive. If someone has closed themselves off in this way, either in business or socially, how can we communicate with them and move forward? It's virtually impossible. These people often fall prey to the high status abusers – just as the weak and vulnerable wildebeest gets picked off by the lions. The high status way of addressing the low status would be to bark such things as 'pull yourself together!' and 'speak up!' Adopting an equally low level of status to communicate would only result in a self-debasement contest.

Again, it is the middle level of status that stands the best chance of getting through. Being open, warm, and approachable will allow the low status access to communicate. It defuses any fear of rebuke. It demonstrates a willingness to engage in a receptive and positive manner. It serves to open channels of communication that can only impact in a good way. Low status individuals can only begin to operate and up their level of status if they are not in fear of reproach or high expectations. Only a middle level of status can give them the opportunity to communicate effectively. If this is practised, the low status individual stands a good chance of functioning in the middle level of status.

5–7 every time!

Stick to the middle

The middle ground of status is unquestionably the way to go. We said that this is about social skills, and that's true, but we need to acknowledge that the right level of status is the absolute bedrock for good communication skills in every area of our lives. Once we assume that we are better or worse than other people we are heading down the wrong track. We must put ourselves in a position to recognize the value of others without backing down or fronting up. The moment we inhabit a status below the 5–7 mark, we are in danger of being subjugated. If we try to establish a high level of status we will never be at an advantage. It's about respect. It's about being sensitive to the needs of other people. If we want to communicate effectively we must learn to listen and respond. We must only feel free to ask the things that will benefit others, or at least be of mutual benefit.

Mine all mine!

A truly charismatic communicator's level of status always gives a great sense of sharing. As theatre director Hilary Wood observed:

'When George Walker Bush took office he looked like he owned The Oval Office, The White House, and Air Force One. When Bill Clinton was in power, he appeared to take ownership of those things on behalf of the American people.'

Stick to the middle of the road and avoid the murky mire on either side. Power and popularity can be achieved through middle status. It is probably true that power and popularity can only be achieved through middle level status. Throughout the centuries, history has thrown up countless powerful figures who have been severely lacking in popularity. To make your way to the top and be generally liked and admired takes a very special quality indeed – charisma. It's far easier to negotiate our way through life with a middle ground status than with anything either side of it. It's much simpler to let people in than cut them off. It's feels a lot better to give and get back rather than to keep and not receive. It's simple!

The menace in the middle

Although the middle channel is definitely where we want to be, there is a rather nasty infection of middle status that we must be on our guard for – manipulative middle. Don't worry too much about this; it's really easy to spot. Once spotted, however, keep a very close eye on it. The manipulative middle abusers are those who appear to be of a confident, open, middle status but are really crafty and two-faced. They will seem to be genuine, sincere and friendly on the surface, but are actually overfriendly and contrived. They will shake you warmly by the hand, probably too warmly and for too long, look you in the eye, again for too long, use your first name several times in one sentence having only just met you, and touch you in a patronizing kind of way (yuk!). It is almost certain that these people will look for an opportunity of selling you down the river at some stage in your relationship with them and then hold out their open palms claiming to be innocent and hurt. Beware!

What a wonderful world

If everyone in the world were to adopt a middle level of status overnight, if we all decided to operate in that

5–7 channel of status – the charisma channel – when we woke up the next morning, the world would be an amazingly pleasant place to live. Relationships would blossom, peace treaties would be signed, the greenhouse effect might be arrested, the hungry would be fed and the world economy would flourish. Life's not like that, is it? But do you know what? We can go a long way to improving our lives and the lives of others simply by adjusting our level of status.

17

Physical status

Radio Rome

Many famous orators of centuries gone by paid great attention to physical fitness. When Cicero went to Rhodes to study under Apollonius Molon, his tutor subjected him to a fitness programme that would make many of today's athletes buckle. 'Speaking in the Forum is comparable to running in a race. It requires stamina and strength,' said Molon. Fortunately, today we have technology to support us. Had Rome's Forum been 'miked up', Cicero may not have felt compelled to stay in such great condition.

The right look

How we look is important, but what we don't want to do in this chapter is to get hung up on clothing, cosmetics, weight, etc. What matters here is how our inner feelings and intentions affect how we are perceived physically. Let's remember that because people see our bodies long before we have eye contact with them or they hear our voice, it is our physical status that makes the first impression. Someone once said that we don't get a second chance at a first impression. We know that's a bit corny but it has its point.

The last thing we want when meeting someone for the first time is to send out the wrong signals physically and have to play catch-up – we don't want people to feel overawed and we don't want to give others the impression that we could be a bit of a pushover either. Let's adopt a failsafe physical status that will support us throughout virtually every situation we are likely to find ourselves in – middle ground status. That's the 5–7 area on the 1–10 scale, you'll recall.

Jack Nicholson once said: 'I don't want people to know what I'm actually like. It's not good for an actor.' Most of us always have to be ourselves, making the best of what we have.

Later in the book is a checklist that keeps us in touch with the best level of physical status.

Comfortable – not arrogant

A proud, confident, straight, relaxed and centred posture will send out the right signals. It will make us more attractive. It will let people know that we mean business in the nicest possible way. It will make others take us seriously but not be afraid to approach. It's the charisma level. Creating the right physical impression is absolutely crucial to getting a relationship off on the right foot. We need people to be interested in us before they know very much about us – we need to send out a message through our physical status that we are accessible and strong; that people can feel confident about establishing a bond with us. The signals may be silent, but the way we carry ourselves has a profound impact on people we may want to cultivate or influence.

The Napoleon complex

A certain self-made businessman, who shall remain nameless, remarkably came to us for presentation coaching (we say remarkably, because it being quite clear that this particular individual had narcissistic tendencies, it was a wonder that he felt he needed any help in the first place). He made an extraordinary statement – he said: 'If I'd been taller I would have been even more successful than I am now.'

No, mister, if you'd been less bent on world domination and adopted a middle-ground status and treated people with the respect they deserved, you'd be even more successful than you are now! This person was short in stature but that certainly wasn't his problem. His problem was the pompous, arrogant, high-handed way he conducted himself in life. He did have a great degree of success in business but was an abject failure where popularity was concerned. None of us wants to be like that. Did Napoleon have a thing about his height or did he just have a big horse?

Getting the right level of physical status

We cannot stress too much how important this is. It might seem obvious for athletes to pay great attention to their physicality, but we should all be doing the same. If we get our status level wrong we will be putting ourselves at a disadvantage from the word go and have the devil's own job getting back to a decent starting point. Working with the right level of physical status is a communication skill that needs to be developed in tandem with every other communication skill to create a great all-round performance.

The body can transmit a wide variety of feelings, attitudes and emotions, and it needs to have a neutral base from which to operate. The body is a vital component to great communication and it is the first thing to come under scrutiny so let's get it right. Once we understand the fundamentals of physical status we will no longer be at a disadvantage when communicating – if we do not understand the subtleties of physical status we will not have an insight into the intentions of others.

In the following sections we will map out what we believe is the best physical starting point as a platform for great communication. Once we have understood and achieved the right level of physical status, great benefits will ensue. Not only will people communicate more readily with us, there will be an increased desire for others to join our company. We will feel physically better and more confident. We will have better balance and move in a more even and fluid way. We might even eradicate certain dull aches and pains that we have been carrying around for years. We will feel more relaxed. We will think more clearly. We will be more alert. People will be warmer and friendlier towards us. We might even begin to get our own way more often. We will feel better about ourselves and we will appear more attractive to those around us. Sounds good? Of course it does. Read on!

Evolution

Man wasn't designed to stand upright and walk on two feet. We would all be much more comfortable if we were running around on all fours. Maybe evolving from the more hirsute primates was not the best thing that could have happened to man. Biologists and physicians will tell us that our frames just aren't up to the job of standing and travelling in a vertical manner. Even after centuries of evolution we are still not getting this standing-up thing right, and back problems probably account for more sick time throughout the world than any other ailment. We are, nevertheless, stuck with it so we might as well make the best of a bad job.

Physical checklist

There is a very simple posture that provides the correct level of physical status for us to enjoy healthy and effective communication. This posture will, when one is used to it, be the most comfortable physical starting point for almost all activity. Here is the checklist:

1 Feet parallel – shoulder-width apart.
2 Legs straight without knees being locked.
3 Pelvis tucked underneath spine – i.e. in a direct line with the spine (our bottoms will always stick out a small amount).
4 Arms hanging loosely by sides.
5 Hands and fingers relaxed.
6 Shoulders relaxed and level.
7 Neck straight and in line with the spine.
8 Head sitting perfectly straight on shoulders facing straight ahead (check chin is not pointing up with head tilting backwards – check chin is not sitting on chest with head lolling forwards).

Napoleon Bonaparte had a fair modicum of success and he was short. We have all heard the expression 'walk tall'. We have another version of that, which is called 'being centred'. In order for us to send out the right physical signals for good communication we do not have to stretch our spines or try to lift our heads off our shoulders. The mid level of physical status (being centred) can be achieved simply by standing erect with our head sitting perfectly centred on level, relaxed shoulders. It really is as simple as that. This status level will send a positive signal across a room before facial expressions can be seen or eye contact established.

It is absolutely crucial to start things off on the right foot. We must always remember that our physicality can say a lot about our state of mind and that people will make subconscious judgements about our character simply from looking at our posture. We need to come across as comfortable and confident so that others will wish to interact with us – 5–7 every time.

Being centred

When actors train, the first thing to be examined is posture. This doesn't mean walking around the room with books balanced precariously on heads – that is probably best left to Swiss finishing schools. It's a matter of finding one's centre, and understanding where that centre is at any point of any piece of communication you are undertaking. Only when an actor is fully familiar with their centre can they begin to explore other physicalities. In order to play a character that has a physical deformity, an actor must have a neutral base to work from and be able to move from that comfortable base to the posture of the character they are playing with reasonable ease. Here are a few examples.

Sir John Mills gave a brilliant Oscar-winning performance as Michael the 'village fool' in David Lean's *Ryan's Daughter* with a facial and physical deformity. Charles Laughton was probably the first screen *Hunchback of Notre Dame*. Daniel Day Lewis adopted an extraordinary twisted posture for his heartrending performance in *My Left Foot,* and on stage Antony Sher's portrayal of *Richard III* was a classic. None of these actors could have achieved these brilliant physical performances if they had not been centred in the first place. Sher's book *Year of the King* gives us an insight into his technique.

Best to stay centred at all times. You will not be dominating and you will not be physically undermined. We are in 5–7 land again. Charisma land. It's a good place to live.

A few tips

- When talking with your partner or children, check your physical status. What is it saying?
- When out shopping, check your status-level with the salesperson assisting you.
- Make sure that you have the same mid-level physical status with your boss and the person beneath you.
- Keep a mid-level status in any social gathering and see the effect it may have on those around you.
- Mid-level physical status will make you feel and look confident and in control. Keep a check on it!

18
Vocal status

If we were to say, 'It's not what you say – it's how you
say it' we would be contradicting everything we said
about story earlier in the book. So, to repeat – what
we say is very important. Getting the story right is
crucial.

It is also vital that we tell our story well and give it
life. If we do not pay attention to the way we sound
we will not achieve this. When we tell stories to our
children we do all sorts of things with our voices that
we would never dream of doing for an adult audience –
what a shame!

Appearance isn't everything

So many people clearly do not pay any attention to the way they sound, but if we were to ask them if they cared about how they sound they would all say, 'Yes, of course I do!' Then why are so many of us not doing anything to improve our vocal image? A great many of the people we are talking about have to stand and speak as part of their jobs, and are probably much more concerned about how they look rather than how they sound. It is very commendable that they are interested in their physical appearance, but that is only one component of a total image. In fact, how people carry themselves physically can have an effect on their vocal image and vice versa – so let's get it right!

Today's technology brings so many facets to our everyday communication and it's important that we are able to embrace the galloping advancements and put them to good use. The great orators of centuries gone by were not so lucky in that sense – they had to rely entirely on physical and vocal technique to get their message across. Let's think – is it really that different today? No, it's not. What is different is the degree of importance we give to maximizing our vocal impact by using modern technology. If anything we should be thinking of technology as merely assisting the hard work we put in on the sound we can make without amplification.

Choice words

Neuro Linguistic Programming (NLP) practitioners will stress the importance of the words we select to communicate and the effect they have on those around us. Isn't it interesting then, how many references we make to sound in our everyday communication? 'I hear what you're saying' … 'I don't like the sound of that' … 'the message was loud and clear' … 'we need to listen to ourselves.'

NLP will tell us that statements like these are sensory word selections. They are, of course, quite instinctive. As soon as we are born, our contact with mother and the outside world is with smell, touch and sound. Even before we can actually focus on an object we start to communicate with sound – 'we find our voice'. We know that if we shout loudly enough we'll get what we want. We grow up experimenting with sound. Sound becomes an enormous part of our lives. We learn by listening and we take our recreation by listening as well. Why is it then, we stop paying attention to the way we sound? It seems crazy.

Put the work in

If we were to have a career in singing we would be training our voices on a daily basis, yet so many people who have to stand and deliver in their business lives do absolutely nothing about the way they sound. It's madness. A professional soccer player will kick footballs every day, even if there isn't a match next week. Golfers will hit balls into a net until their hands blister just to get their swings working well. They do it because their livelihood depends on it. It is thought that managers in business will spend 80 per cent of their day communicating verbally. Isn't it then absolutely essential that they not only care about how they sound, but that they do something to improve the way they sound? Of course it is!

Everyone knows that they can achieve more if how they say something has the 'right ring to it'. The voice is a very powerful and expressive instrument with a great range of sounds. We must never underestimate the power and control we can exert through our voice alone. Making a good first impression by getting our physical status right is very important. Backing up that physical status by working on how we sound is just as important if not more so. We have all had the experience of 'good' or 'bad' teaching because of the quality and use of the voices of our teachers. Teaching is certainly one profession where the importance of vocal delivery is paramount – teachers are, after all, helping to shape the lives of our children.

'Words mean more than what is set down on paper. It takes the human voice to infuse them with deeper meaning' is how Maya Angelou put it. And 'Lord, what an organ is human speech when played on by a master.' That was Mark Twain's opinion.

A lone voice

What happens when we are not able to use our physicality? What happens when we are not able to make that first impression through appearance and the effective use of body language? What happens when we cannot be seen? Many people earn their living by being heard but not seen. Recording artists are the most obvious, and the enjoyment of listening to them plays a huge part in our lives – but what about the announcers on TV and radio? What about the excitement created by the commentator on our favourite ball game, or the frustration we suffer when we cannot understand what the man is telling us about the train on platform two? What happens every time we pick up the telephone?

There are countless thousands if not millions of businesses throughout the world that rely solely on telephone sales, yet they appear to give absolutely no vocal training to their sales force. They actually appear to care little or nothing about the content and their story either, but let's not go into that! Have you ever had a bad experience at the hands of a company's switchboard operator? We know you have. How many times have you spoken to someone in business who couldn't give a damn whether you do business with them or not, or certainly sounded like they didn't? Plenty, no doubt. Sound and vocal image is so important to our charisma.

Cheer up, it might never happen

We recently did some work for a rather prominent events organizer. Their automated telephone system ebulliently boasted that they were 'the organizers of the most exciting corporate events!' – yet when you pressed 0 for an operator you might as well have been talking to 'Fred's Funeral Parlour'.

Some time ago we needed to make arrangements by phone to carry out some group work for a major automobile manufacturer. The voice on the end of the line was monotonous, and appeared completely uninterested in what we needed to do. This was the voice of their Director of Communications! What on earth is going on? It simply isn't good enough. These people must be losing business hand over fist.

If the success of your company depends on great telephone technique, spend some money on training your staff to send out the right company image, and that means learning how to make the best of your voice; and at least sound vaguely interested in what you are doing. The difference between someone sounding bright, positive and happy to receive your call, and the negative, abrupt, 'couldn't care less' approach, could be someone hanging up and going elsewhere and the acquisition of a major contract – and it starts with the person who answers the phone.

Sounds good

All of this might sound obvious, but so many businesses are getting it wrong. It is quite possible for a company to bumble along for years doing 'OK' when they should probably be doing really well. This could be down to how the company promotes itself generally or, equally, it might be due to the attitude and sound of the person on reception. Either way, those people managing the company need to look at the vocal image projected by those they employ. It's not difficult and it's worth investing in.

Getting the right level of vocal status and projecting a good vocal image is equally important in our private lives. The sound we make when talking to our partner or our children can mean the difference between enjoying peace and harmony, or living in an atmosphere of knife-edge tension. It really is as basic as that. The more we think about the effect our voice is having on other people, the more capable we will be at creating a productive and pleasant environment to live in. So, wouldn't it be great if not only our career prospects looked good but our domestic and social lives were also flourishing because we had found an understanding of vocal status and improved our vocal image? We must also remind ourselves that a good vocal image will count for nothing if we have not learned to listen properly. Great communication is about listening and responding – the charismatic way.

High vocal status

'He loves the sound of his own voice!' How many times have we heard that?

There are those who talk 'nineteen to the dozen' and appear to have a lot to say for themselves but could not be considered high status. There are also those who raise their chins and pontificate, or simply 'talk down their noses' at us. Never quite sure which is more irritating? There are so many phrases that apply directly to high vocal status:

'You can hear her a mile away.'

'He's full of hot air.'

'Her bark's worse than her bite.'

'He's such an old windbag!'

If we thought those kind of remarks were being said about us, we would, of course, be mortified. People would not only find what we have to say a turn-off, but they would also find the way we said it unpalatable and irritating – and they'd probably be right.

Pompous bluster, arrogant rhetoric, high-volume righteous reproach are generally accompanied by tones of self-adoration. They are not attractive and they are counterproductive. It's not big, it's not clever but it can be quite funny. People who operate this high vocal status are often ridiculed and made figures of fun. If we look at some well-known situation comedies we can see how writers make great use of high-status characters when writing their dialogue. Captain Mainwaring in *Dad's Army* and Basil Fawlty in *Fawlty Towers* are at their most comic when delivering their dialogue with bombastic pomposity. Both characters succeed because of their high level of vocal status – anyone applying this in real life is sure to fail.

We were once asked to stand at the back of a room where a senior business figure was addressing a gathering of journalists to see if we could identify ways in which he could make his delivery 'even more dynamic' than it already was (his words apparently). The gentleman concerned went to great lengths to let his audience know that he wanted the meeting to be informal and that he would welcome any questions and comments they might have. Sure enough one journalist took him at his word and posed a question to which the 'dynamic' businessman barked back:

'This is a speech not a conversation!'

Needless to say, the remark and the ferocity with which it was delivered did him no favours and he was torn apart by the pack. What he said would have been a great line for Basil or Captain Mainwaring, and we would all have been quoting it with great fondness for many years to come. Not quite so with the newspapers.

The doctor will see you now

Some doctors' receptionists can dish out a nasty line in vocal high status. Many of us have been victims of the sharp tongues that separate us from the people who can save our lives and many people have, no doubt, changed surgery because of it. Why do people do it? It is so damaging and unnecessary, especially in this kind of situation where people are vulnerable and not at their best. Maybe being in positions of power where people can prey upon those at risk and in need of help attracts a certain type. Maybe there's a special training school for officious receptionists and PAs, where they are taught to parry any innocent enquiries with vicious attacks. Who knows?

There is absolutely no room for high vocal status in good communication. Let's remember that certain forms of high vocal status are only a step away from physical violence. There are three ways in which vocal high status is dealt with:

● Retreating and curling up into a ball for self-protection.

- Bottling up the anger and eventually lashing out.
- Meeting it with a neutral vocal status (more about that later).

It's perfectly safe to say that great communicators do not employ a high vocal status. Mid-level vocal status is without doubt the failsafe and most effective level to operate at.

Low vocal status

At the other end of the status scale is another no-no. We all make judgements about people because of the sounds they make, and listening to low vocal status can be just as much a turn-off as having high vocal status inflicted upon us.

One could almost come down in favour of the high vocal status – well, at least we can hear it! Sorry – that's a little facetious, but you know what we mean. Of course, low vocal status is not just about volume, but being able to hear what someone is saying is pretty essential to good communication. In the same way that the volume of some high vocal status people can push us away, straining to catch what a person is saying will also have a negative effect. We are all, by and large, polite people and we will endeavour to make sure we listen to what a person has to say and respond accordingly. If the speaker is making it difficult for us to hear them, we will eventually become too embarrassed to keep asking them to repeat themselves, give up trying to hear them and stop communicating all together. Good communication must be fluid, and low volume low vocal status goes directly against that and closes us down. All sounds rather simplistic doesn't it? So why do we do it and why do we allow it to happen?

Don't sink to their level

Volume aside, there is another more disturbing manifestation of low vocal status which we all need to be aware of: low vocal status manipulation. In Chapter 16 we spoke about low status manipulation and its dangers. Now we can pinpoint and recognize the sounds low status manipulators use. The self-deprecating running-down will invariably be done in whining, almost hushed tones. The bolstering 'admiration' of others will be delivered at a slightly higher volume, in a simpering kind of way. Do not fall prey to this kind of assault (for that is what it is) because it will bleed you dry. It will sap you until your own status is heading down to join it. Beware!

Children are particularly good at low vocal status manipulation, and many of them carry this strategy into their adult lives where it is performed with much less 'innocent' intentions. Cocking one's head to one side and speaking in a higher register voice is not cute in adults – it is done for a reason, which is devious and calculating. It is intended to catch you off guard and bring about an early capitulation. Children employ this tactic to obtain treats. The grown-up low vocal status abuser is playing for much higher stakes. When employing a childlike voice backfires, the speaker will simply come across as insecure and we will have no confidence in them.

When manipulative low vocal status is used in telephone conversations it can be particularly deadly. We don't have the benefit of reading the body language, and that can make it more difficult to identify and tackle. It's always best to fight in the open where we can see what's happening. Dealing with this kind of approach on the phone can be a nightmare – yes, we could hang up but we're too nice for that so we continue the conversation at a disadvantage, being worn down bit by bit. Sound familiar?

Mid-level vocal status

The charisma level is memorably defined by Rudyard Kipling:

If you can talk with crowds and keep your virtue,
Or walk with kings – nor lose the common touch …

Oh yes, this is the stuff! It's comfortable. It feels really good. It has the right effect and it fits perfectly with our mid-level physical status. No timid apologies and no deafening arrogance. We don't have to speak softly and we don't have to carry a big stick. We just have to listen and respond with a calm and measured thought and a clarity of speech at an acceptable volume. Easy!

No, of course it's not that easy. Just like everything else in life we have to work at it, especially when we have probably paid it little or no attention at all – but it can be done and it will have an extremely positive impact on our lives and on the lives of those we come into contact with. Sounds ideal. Sounds impossible! Well, let's take a look at some examples of mid-level status in action.

Is there a doctor in the house?

One of the great things about offering a service like ours is that anyone can use it, and consequently we have the pleasure of working with a wide variety of people and professions. The National Health Service and its employees offers a great example of how effective mid-level status can be and, of course, how damaging adopting the wrong level of status can be when it comes to caring for people. We all know what a good and a bad bedside manner is – or do we?

Hitting the right level of vocal status when dealing with the sick is essential for speeding up their recovery and improving their well-being. Going for the Sir Lancelot Spratt approach as portrayed by James Robertson Justice in the film *Doctor in the House* is unlikely to ingratiate any doctor to those in their care – patients cannot be intimidated into getting better. There are some doctors who will stand by the bedside speaking with a high vocal status to a group of trainee doctors about patients as if they weren't even there. By the same token a low status approach will not give patients confidence in their doctor's abilities, which will add to their anxiety and possibly worsen their condition. Now we can see how important it is for people in the medical profession to get this vocal status business right.

When discussing this subject with a good friend who also happens to be a general practitioner, he put forward an interesting theory about patient recovery. He believes that the body stands the best chance of working its own magic if a patient is comfortable and happy. Well, that certainly makes sense. Patients can only be comfortable and happy, however, if they are being treated with care and respect and not being barked at or talked down to or having to strain to hear what is being said about them. We are talking about a good bedside manner: a mid-level status that listens and responds with a good vocal image. Our GP friend has no doubt that the way in which doctors communicate with their patients is equally as important as the treatment they give to them.

Sound the alarm!

Fire-fighters and paramedics tend to have the right level of vocal status. Their vocal status has to be such that the people they are helping feel reassured and safe, otherwise their jobs would be so much harder. They know that the people they are saving could go into shock at any moment and not recover, so they have to instil in them a feeling of comfort and trust. Only a mid-level vocal status can achieve this. If the right level of vocal status can have the desired effect in these extreme circumstances, think what it could do for us in our everyday lives.

We mentioned teachers earlier in this chapter. One of our great experiences with the teaching profession has been with one of our coaches who is a teacher turned actor/director. In the 25 years we have know him we have never seen him outside of that 5–7 status bracket except when exploring status on stage. His talent and adopted level of status (especially vocal status) are a potent combination that equips him to get performances out of people they never thought themselves capable of. He is a brilliant example of the positive effect that mid-level vocal status can have on those we have to connect with.

The scenery is better on the radio

Radio and TV presenters were also referred to earlier in this chapter, and on radio the voice is the only instrument of communication they have. 'Television contracts the imagination and radio expands it' once declared Sir Terry Wogan, a shining beacon of mid-level vocal status. His soft, mellifluous, dimple-inducing banter made him BBC Radio 2's favourite for over a quarter of a century – doing a brilliant job aided by middle-level vocal status.

Fall the men in Sergeant Wilson!

Will Scully – an ex-Special Forces serviceman, recently decorated with the Queen's Gallantry Medal for mounting a single-handed mission to rescue 1,400 tourists from the hands of blood-thirsty rebels in Sierra Leone (read his book *Once a Pilgrim*) is a great example of mid-level vocal status. If you were to have a conversation with Scully you would never guess that he was a man capable of such an enormously heroic feat; he would simply be someone you felt drawn to and comfortable with. Colonel Tim Collins, now famous for his Shakespearean-style speech to his men at their camp in the desert just hours before they went into battle, is another fantastic example of someone who has used his mid-level vocal status with great effect. Everything about Col. Tim is 5–7 charisma channel, and now when he speaks to audiences all over the world they understand why his men were willing to do anything he asked of them and why they had the utmost respect for the people they were engaging in battle. Here are two people who have had to work under very difficult conditions and achieved great things by staying in that mid-channel – they definitely have charisma.

John McCarthy – the British journalist taken hostage in Beirut in April 1986 – seems to inhabit that mid-level status area very comfortably. We can never imagine McCarthy getting on the high end of vocal status: it doesn't appear to fit with his character. This may well have stood him in good stead during more than five years of incarceration.

Let's do ourselves a favour and take a good look at our vocal image. Who knows – it might even save our lives one day.

Admirable Nelson

Nelson Mandela – one of the world's best-loved political figures – is a wonderful exponent of mid-level vocal status. If there is anyone in the world entitled to have a serious attitude problem it is Nelson Mandela, but when he speaks we never feel that we are being lectured to or having a finger wagged at us. We see a man who appears comfortable with himself and happy with his life. We see someone we would feel very much at ease with. In spite of being wrongfully imprisoned for most of his life we simply see a man speaking passionately from his heart. He once said: 'It is better to lead from behind and to put others in front, especially when you celebrate victory when nice things occur. You take the front line when there is danger. Then people will appreciate your leadership.'

It is interesting to note that Bill Clinton, another charismatic communicator, is a very good friend of Mandela and visits South Africa every year for Nelson's birthday party.

Tackling low

Mid-level vocal status is definitely where we need to be. If we are dealing with someone who is employing low vocal status, whether it be in volume or tone or even if it is trying to be manipulative, we need to stick rigidly to our mid-level vocal status. It's a secure anchor and it is very possible that we could, with persistence, raise the vocal status level of the person were are engaging with and have a more meaningful interaction.

Tackling high

'Stop shouting at me!!' The last thing we want to do when handling someone's extreme high vocal status is match them. Once again we need to hang on to our mid-level status come what may. This will let the assailant know that you are not intimidated and that they need to drop their level or look silly. Honestly – it really works. Try it – you won't be disappointed.

The centre path

Mid-level vocal status will give you confidence, dignity and appeal. Don't even think of going anywhere else. Whether you are dealing with a difficult person at work, giving a public address or talking to the kids, it's where you need to be.

So, let's take a look at our vocal image as it is now and how we would like it to be.

PTSV – Pitch/Tone/Speed/Volume
Pitch

Let's not fool ourselves into thinking that we are suddenly going to have a voice like Richard Burton, Orson Welles or Joanna Lumley. Let's develop our voices by finding our natural pitch. That means the pitch of voice we are most comfortable with. It will be somewhere in the middle of our range. Pitching it right is very important for our own comfort, and very often our natural pitch is not the one we find ourselves using.

Some people seek to change the pitch of their voice (usually lowering it) to make themselves sound more sexy, appealing or authoritative. Margaret Thatcher did exactly this (to sound appealing) before she became Prime Minister – she lowered the pitch and softened her delivery. Do you really want to do that? If you do want to change the natural pitch of your voice, you need to ask yourself exactly why you want to change it, and don't settle for anything other than a very valid reason. If you find a good reason then seek the help of a voice specialist.

This book is not going to help those who wish to speak in a pitch that is an octave below the pitch that is natural to them; we are only interested in helping you to find the pitch that is most comfortable to you. Keith Waterhouse once remarked that Margaret Thatcher always sounded as though she was talking to someone whose dog has just died. Maybe it's best to stick with what we've got!

Recognizing and strengthening our natural pitch will improve our everyday communication. It will also serve as a platform from which we can vary our pitch to emphasize certain points and give texture to our speaking voice. We must also remember that the pitch of our voice will change naturally, depending on how we feel about what we are saying. When the pitch does vary naturally it will be supported with sufficient breath and our voices will be safe.

Stop thief!

If you were sitting at home and you happened to glance out of the window to see someone stealing your car, you would probably shout 'Hey!!' at great volume and in a higher pitch than your natural speaking voice. When you are vocalizing naturally and instinctively, your breathing mechanism will support your voice automatically. If you decide to change the natural pitch of your voice without expert guidance, you run the risk of doing serious damage to your vocal cords. Be careful; our voices are our primary instrument of communication and they need to be looked after properly.

If we start to impose things on our natural voice falsely, we will sound 'phoney'. So far as we are aware, the expression 'phoney' did not arise from the mistrust of what people were being told on the telephone when they could not see the person they were talking to. Oh, we wish it did, because it so precisely describes a trap we can all too easily fall into. Do we want to appear 'phoney'? No, of course not. So we must guard against using an unnatural voice. We won't be believed even if we can be seen! We don't want that – it's a total turn-off and people probably won't believe a word we are saying, and who'd blame them. There is a suggestion that the origin of 'phoney' may be from the Irish *fainne*, a ring, from the old practice of tricking people into buying gilt rings which they believed to be genuine gold.

Everyone's voice is unique. Some people speak in a high register, others speak in a low register. Somewhere in the middle of the register will be your natural pitch. Once you have found your natural pitch you can explore the notes either side of that pitch for a more interesting delivery.

Tone

'Don't take that tone of voice with me!'

Did your parents ever say that to you? Of course they did. The tone of our voices is extremely important for good communication. Choosing the right tone for the right situation can mean the difference of winning or losing, or life and death. Think back to the captivity of John McCarthy in Beirut. Remember the real-life negotiators who hold people's lives in their hands. Getting the tone right is absolutely crucial.

Artists will use different tones of colour, like light and shade in a painting to illustrate what they are seeing. We must use our voices like the artists use their palettes to tell our stories.

Tone is about resonance and intention. When our parents snapped at us for 'taking that tone' we had clearly upset them, and maybe that was what we intended to do. The tones we choose to speak with are chosen to have an effect on those we are talking to.

People who use the extremes of vocal status tend to have tones that irritate us. The timid, slightly whiny tone of the low vocal status and the unpleasant, cocky tones of the high vocal status grate upon the ears and make us unwilling listeners. A rather grand British actor taking the waters in a Wimbledon pub was overheard to say:

'No, darling I turned the role down, it wasn't my tonality.'

The irritating tone of pompous arrogance. Yuk! High status at its worst. Let's hope his 'tonality' didn't appear too often on the stages of London's West End.

God! He's so boring!

One tone that can operate at the high or low level is the dreaded monotone. Irritating vocal tones will make the listener switch off, and the monotone is probably the worst of the bunch. People can be as enthusiastic as they wish about any subject they want, but if they have a monotonous voice they might as well keep quiet about it. Nobody wants to listen to monotones; they get on our nerves and even make us feel hostile to the person speaking.

Soon changed her tune

Your voice is such a powerful tool it can affect people in many ways, and tone has a lot to do with it. This is why it is so important that we listen to ourselves and be selective about the tones we use for different situations. We also need to listen to the tones of other people that we find annoying and question if we use the same tones. If you think you do then you must do something about it. Change your tones. It won't sound phoney, and it could improve or even save your life. The warm tones we choose to use within our natural pitch will make it easier for people to listen to us; get our message across and make people want to communicate with us.

Let's remember how important getting the right tone is with some of the professions we spoke about earlier – the soldier, the nurse, the fire-fighter, the paramedic, the negotiator – the success of these people is largely down to the tones they choose to communicate with, and we should be just as aware about that fact as they are. There will be times when we need to step outside of the middle channel with our tones to achieve the desired effect but, by and large, the mid-level vocal status will serve us well.

Let's keep listening to ourselves.

Speed

The speed at which we speak is very important for good communication, and once again the mid-level vocal pace is the winner. Some people speak very slowly, which can make us switch off in frustration. We might even feel that we are being patronized by a slow delivery. We might feel that the speaker thinks that what they have to say is enormously interesting and that we will be hanging on their every word. We just want to receive the information more quickly so we can resume our usual pace of life. Whatever it is that makes someone speak overly slowly, it almost invariably has a negative effect on the listener. Fortunately, it is only a very small percentage of people who speak too slowly – a much larger percentage of people speak too quickly.

She talks nineteen to the dozen

It's a strange expression but we know what it means. Machinegunfire speech can be just as frustrating for the listener as a laboured delivery, but it is easier to understand why some people speak faster than we would like them to, especially when they are speaking in public and anxiety kicks in.

There are reasons other than anxiety for rapid speech. Some people have very fast and agile minds that jump around like grasshoppers. They are already on to the next bit before they've finished the bit they were doing. We must live in the now. We cannot expect our audience to keep up with us if we don't give them a chance – it's not fair and they will switch off. Once we understand why we are speaking too quickly we can do something about it.

We once worked with a very bright woman, who was head of HR for a major TV broadcaster, and who was probably the fastest speaker we have ever encountered. It took some time to discover why she was like this but eventually we found out. She was the youngest of five sisters. When they were growing up, personal speaking time was at a premium. She told us that whenever there was a gap in their conversation, one of them had to jump in and get out what she wanted to say as quickly as possible before someone else took their turn. Of course, she carried this into her adult life. Again, once we found out why she spoke so rapidly we were a long way to curing the problem.

Errr...

Perhaps this is a good time to talk about audible pauses. The ums and ers that we pepper our speaking with. Not so bad in everyday conversation, but in a speech or a presentation they are very irritating indeed. As soon as we understand why we do it we can do something about stopping it happening. We do it in conversation because we feel that we need to fill those gaps or someone else will jump in and take our turn at speaking. It's true! That's the reason – and it's subconscious. When we stand up to make a speech or a presentation we are much less likely to have that problem. So instead of filling in the gaps with ums and ers, leave them empty. Audible pauses are not attractive – real pauses are great and, believe it or not, it is very interesting watching someone who isn't speaking!

Back up to speed

We must speak at a pace our audience can keep up with which, for most of us, will mean slowing down to a pace that probably feels laboured, dull and uncomfortable. It won't come across as laboured or dull; it will almost certainly be just right. Get someone to listen to you speaking – ask their opinion of whether you are too quick or too slow. Once you have the pace that your audience can be comfortable with and absorb what you are telling them – then you can vary the pace, give light and shade to your delivery and make the way you present information and ideas more interesting.

Volume

The problem is like being too quick or too slow, only this time it's too loud or too quiet.

There is the story of the two rival actors at a friend's birthday party, both with huge voices trading insults from different rooms. It was a long and bitter battle before one delivered the killer blow:

'Is it true you began your theatrical career in the circus where a lion had to put its head in your mouth?'

Can you hear me at the front?

'Get on, say the wordies loud and clear, and get off.' Good advice from actress Pamela Brown.

The best place for booming theatrical voices is on the stage. Although actors attempt to hold the mirror up to nature, they can, on occasions, let the play run away with them and 'over resonate'. Because the theatre situation is not a natural one we can forgive them and even enjoy a big performance. Some of today's younger actors have been criticized for mumbling on stage and not being heard. Sir Peter Hall, who founded the Royal Shakespeare Company said recently:

'Actors now think that if they raise their voice, they are being "unrealistic". I tell them: "What you do is unreal. You're wearing someone else's clothes and speaking someone else's words".'

The same is not true in life outside the theatre and we must be conscious of the volume we use in our communications. We need our audiences to be comfortable with the volume of sound we are giving.

Whenever we have any presentation skills training we will invariably be told to speak up. Yes, it is important that we can be heard but it is also important that we don't overdo it. We must listen to ourselves and ask the opinion of others about how we speak. It is very unlikely that we will find ourselves in a situation where we are asked to speak without amplification but we do, nevertheless, need to produce sufficient volume for the mike to pick up. If we deliver a muffled utterance, the microphone will amplify and muffle the utterance. Just like everyone else in the room, we will be able to hear and adjust the level of amplification if necessary. We must listen to ourselves.

The biggest danger, when it comes to volume, is not being heard. This occurs when low vocal status is in action as mentioned before. If we cannot be heard we might as well not bother speaking at all. It really is as simple as that. There are a number of reasons why people find it difficult to make themselves heard and a lack of confidence in their ability to communicate is the main one. Confidence comes when all the components of good communication are working together as one – the 'communicating with charisma' way. We can be painfully shy but still operate as good communicators when we take the trouble to piece together the elements we need to connect effectively. Finding your natural speaking voice can be very empowering. Go for it!

The right vocal status

The right vocal status will make us accessible. The right vocal status will mirror everything that is good about the right level of physical status. What we really want to achieve by getting our vocal status where we need it to be is, *when others find it desirable to communicate with us.* That's all. If we achieve that goal, people will listen to us and what we have to say might have a positive effect on them. What more can we ask?

If we have that charisma level of status – open warm, receptive, approachable and strong – every area of our lives will flourish. We won't be the canny businessperson

Vocal status

117

who makes millions but their family finds them difficult to connect with. We won't be the Mr or Mrs Nice Person who hides their light under a bushel and never gets what they want. We won't spend a miserable life avoiding speaking obligations. We will enjoy productive personal development. We will be more attractive to those around us. We will have opened the gate to a whole new world of positive personal interaction.

19

Emotional status

When things are steep remember to stay level headed.
Horace (Quintus Horatius Flaccus 65–8 BC:
Roman poet)

Some years ago during one of The Speechworks staff training sessions we were stressing the importance of working with status, when one of our coaches made an interesting observation. We were naturally keen to emphasize that all areas of status must be covered; physical, mental and vocal, but it was pointed out to us that we had failed to address emotional status. Is there such a thing? Doesn't that come under mental status?

The fundamental factor

Although our training day had only just started we spent the rest of the day discussing emotional status.

Yes, not only does it exist but it is probably the most important area of the subject of status, and yes, it does fall into the mental category especially with regard to the management of emotion. Emotional status is at the very core of all our communication – it is the inner-artist's palette – it is the tool that shapes 'communicating with charisma'. If we develop our emotional skills we are going to live happier and more successful lives. We will function with a greater clarity of thought and enjoy more productive relationships. We will operate with empathy and a better understanding of other people's needs. We will be able to stay focused on what is important in our working and personal lives. Emotional status is the key to the success of every piece of human interaction.

Emotional understanding

Understanding our own emotions gives us a greater insight into the moods and desires of other people, and allows us to make the right decisions about how to react appropriately to them. Not only will it help us manage our own performance – it will also give us the ability to steer the behaviour of those around us and create win-win situations. Logically applied, management of emotions will equip us to make choices that will enrich our business, social and domestic lives.

Beware the dark side of the force!

At the risk of banging on about the extremes of status, we do need to stress the dangers of operating under the 'dark side' or, indeed, the 'somewhat too light side' of the emotional spectrum. The outer limits will, of course, close us down for meaningful communication. Anger and rage are not agents of positive communication – they will only serve to push people away with no desire to resume normal service. Obsessive worrying is the route to an unattractive anxiety disorder. Over-enthusiastic, forever smiley behaviour will probably be considered glib or flippant, and will certainly not be taken seriously. Deeply sincere hand-holding concern will be greeted with mistrust. Neglecting to exercise some control over the extremes of emotion will get in the way of our ability to focus clearly on what we are doing. Another quote from Kipling's 'If –' is apposite here: 'If you can keep your head when all about you are losing theirs …'

Those people who are attuned to their emotions and who are able to manage the extremes recover from setbacks far more quickly and are able to get on with enjoying their lives. We know that life in business is fraught with people problems, obstacles that need to be negotiated and rejections that must be coped with. People in sales can suffer rejection on a frequent basis and have to have techniques and strategies for dealing with that. Those that allow the emotional extremes that can result from rejection to set in are sure to be out-sold by a sales staff in command of their emotional status.

Let's get this thing right! Again – not rocket science, so why do so many of us get it wrong so much of the time?

Maybe we get it wrong because we have not been aware of how wonderful things can be when we concentrate on getting it right. Perhaps we get too tied up in ourselves to reap the benefits of understanding and focusing on the needs and desires of others.

The need for empathy

Empathy begins in infancy. Small children empathize naturally. We've all seen children cry because another child is crying. They are simply attuning to the feelings of the child in distress. They have made an emotional connection. It's instinctive – in order for children to be happy they need to be in an emotionally stable environment which extends to the feelings of other children around them. Children develop this skill quite naturally. As we get older, and our lives become more cluttered, we tend to lose some of this innate ability.

The bigger picture

We need to be empathetic if we are going to be successful, and only a clear understanding of our own emotions is going to allow that to happen. Emotions are good and without them life would be very dull indeed, so let's not suppress our emotions. We need to examine our feelings. We have to be sure that our feelings are real and not what we want them to be. We have to understand that what we feel at the moment isn't necessarily what we might feel in two minutes' time. We need to check our feelings and make sure that they are true. When we can do this, we can recognize the true feelings of others and empathize with them.

Anyone who ignores the need for empathy and continues to bash down the road to their own success regardless of the feelings of other people will lose out because they are not seeing the bigger picture. It's important that we understand our emotions so we can be attuned to the feelings of those around us. Interpersonal understanding is the very cornerstone of a happy and successful life. It will maintain the balance needed to steer a true and harmonious course through our business, domestic and social lives.

People skills

We've all heard about these. People skills are all about being empathetic. If we are not sensitive to the feelings of others we do not have people skills. This is where great charismatic communicators score so highly. They have the leadership qualities that are born out of genuine empathy. They have the ability to bring people together to resolve differences; an instinctive nose for the requirements and desires of other people; a capacity to listen and respond to the worries and concerns of those around them and a capability to interpret the mood and react accordingly. This is what sets them apart from the rest. These are the emotional skills that help give them charisma.

We few, we happy few, we band of brothers ...

Some time ago we found ourselves working with a very talented and high-ranking business figure from the world of finance – let's call him Simon. Nothing unusual there you might think, and you'd be right except for one thing. Many years prior to getting in touch with us, Simon had subconsciously decided to cut himself off emotionally from almost all of his dealings with other people, and he only became properly aware of this when he went on a leadership course in Austria. This was a very expensive course led by an eminent clinical psychologist. Part of one of the exercises on the course was to recall three emotional events in his life and recount them, which he duly did. The psychologist found his choice of events very interesting, and remarked that they had all taken place over twenty years ago and he was now in his mid-forties – so where had he been for the last twenty years? He had married, had children and had lost members of his family. Surely these were huge emotional events?

As a result of this discovery, Simon began to understand some of the criticism aimed at him by his colleagues about his not being passionate about pretty much anything. His first concern was how he behaved at home. Did he give and share himself properly with his family? After careful thinking he felt confident that he showed the warmth and love for his family that he naturally should. Delving further he felt fairly comfortable that he engaged in the right way socially.

He was concerned deeply, however, when he thought about the people who relied upon him in his business life. Yes, he got the job done. Yes, he was dependable. But did he connect properly with the people who depended upon him? Was he in touch with their needs? Was he letting them in? Did it matter? Yes it did, and he desperately wanted to change how he was perceived. He wanted to be that open, strong, inspiring yet caring leader that his people could go to. He felt that he needed to be the special figure that people felt happy and safe with, and wanted to do their best for. He wanted to be there for them in every way.

When we began to work with him, this desire to be passionate and enthusiastic about what he did and the people that helped him do it were at the top of his list. Part of the programme we embarked upon was looking at great inspiring and caring leaders throughout history, and one day we took a look at a couple of film clips of Henry V – one was delivered by Laurence Olivier and the other by Kenneth Branagh. Simon seemed to be drawn to both performances and when they were over he said, 'I want to be him!' We were not sure which actor he meant: 'No no...' he said, 'I want to be Henry V!'

Simon was booked to give the keynote speech at a global conference in Atlanta, US, and was using the time we spent together to prepare. Part of the preparation was to work on the St Crispin's Day speech from Henry V. He was one of those people who spent a large part of his life on planes dashing here and there, taking care of his people around the world, and we never thought that we would actually see him give his Henry V until one special day in his company's board room in the City of London. He apologized for not having spent too much time on the piece because of travel and pressures of work, but he was excited and determined to give it a go. What followed was astonishing. We were treated to a word-perfect performance of such depth, understanding and passion it made us gasp. It was a performance that would not have been out of place on stage at the National Theatre.

Shortly afterwards we saw a DVD of his keynote speech at the conference – performed without notes or slides to a spellbound audience. There was no way back for Simon – he had made the emotional investment that was needed in his communications that set him apart from other people. He had mined, refined and delivered his charisma!

Caring, listening and reacting empathically are at the root of happier and more productive lives. We are all capable of it. We can all read the body language that gives away emotion – the look, the gesture, the posture, the tone of voice. We just need to take the time to access our own emotions and attune to the feelings of others.

Listen and share

If we think about the people we are drawn to, they are usually the ones in touch with and in control of their emotions. They are invariably the people who seem interested in us, listen well and make us feel good. They know what makes us tick and are able to press all our happy buttons. What a quality! It is hard to be jealous of these people – they are too easy to like – and do you know what? We can be just like them with a little application.

We must never forget that displays of emotion will always have an effect on other people, so we must monitor ours and be ready to read and empathize with others. We all know people who always seem to be there for us, people we can rely on, people we trust, people who consider our feelings, people who listen! These are the people we gravitate towards, these are the people we find attractive, and these are the people we want to be with. They have charisma, and the reason they have charisma is because they are accessible, in control and attuned to the needs of others – they share themselves with us and make us feel special. A lot of people may have this quality naturally, but we are all capable of recognizing it and developing it in ourselves.

Building a rapport

Knowing how other people are feeling helps us to create a rapport. Understanding and managing emotion in ourselves and others is a skill we need to learn and hone if we are going to improve life for ourselves and those we come into contact with. This is the skill of the leader bringing people together to work as one. This is the skill of the negotiator resolving the differences of warring factions or interacting with hostage takers. This is the skill of the good salesperson sensing what is right for the customer and building long-term relationships. This is the skill of the military commanders who are responsible for the lives of their troops. This is the skill of the nurse who understands what it takes to help a patient make a speedy recovery. These may seem obvious positions where good management of emotion is crucial, but whatever we do and even when we are at home or out with friends we can all be more sensitive to our emotional status. On p. 129 there is a checklist to see how we can improve our interpersonal performance with regard to emotional status.

A good old weepy

When we are at the theatre or cinema we expect our emotions to be touched in some way by what we see on the stage or on the screen. We are happy to let our guard down and give ourselves up to the whole gamut of the emotional spectrum; in fact, we kind of expect to have our emotions pulled apart. Fear, anxiety, sadness, joy are all par for the course in that short period of time. It is the job of the actors, writers and directors to use their emotional skills to steer our emotional status. This conscious management of an audience's emotions is no different when embarking on any form of communication.

Emotion at the podium

The moment we stand up to speak we have the opportunity to change the feelings of our audience by demonstrating how we feel about the subject we are speaking about. We must decide how we want our audience to feel when we have finished speaking. Their emotions are very much in our control. There is probably one overriding feeling that we must always leave our audiences feeling no matter what the subject – hope.

A politician's vision, the plea on behalf of a charitable organization, the heartfelt words of the bride's father – all of these examples of a speaker's subject matter should leave us with a sense of hope. A hope that if we vote for him or her that things will get better. A hope that our donation will give food to the starving. A hope that the newly-weds will live happily ever after.

Hope throughout history

Hope seems to be an underlying theme in many forms of public address, and no more so than some of the most famous speeches in history. Churchill's 'fight them on the beaches' speech, Martin Luther King's 'I have a dream' speech, Bill Clinton's acceptance speech for the Democrat's nomination, and Barack Obama's nomination speech are all laced with hope. Even some of the rallying addresses of the Third Reich were about hope. Hope is probably the best, almost failsafe, feeling to send an audience home with – it's positive, upbeat and optimistic. Leading up to the hopeful ending a speaker can evoke a whole series of different emotions, taking an audience on a journey of ever-changing emotional status. Again, just like in the theatre or cinema, it is what we expect from the experience and the skill of the performer, in being able to move and influence an audience in this way – especially when an audience believes that they have witnessed the speaker's true feelings.

Sensing the mood

The great speakers of history, from Demosthenes to JFK, have been able to sense an audience's feelings and respond to them. The best communicators are those who are sensitive to the mood of the crowd. Churchill, King, Hitler were all able to create and shape the emotional journey of their audiences. All of them honing and developing their craft with every speech. Even the great Roman orator Cicero saw the need to refine, rehearse and be trained in the art of speechmaking. Some of the greats were natural-born communicators but they also recognized the need to improve their skills. Once we are in tune with our emotions and the emotions of other people and are prepared to put in the time, we too can obtain the power of a good speaker.

How sensitive are we?

As a starting point, how do we measure up to Mark Twain's dictum:

'Good breeding consists in concealing how much we think of ourselves and how little we think of other persons.'

We need to monitor as many different pieces of communication as we can to see if we are managing our emotions and the emotional status of those in any given situation and environment. Below is a checklist to help us out.

More listening

- Do we really listen to other people?
- Have we already decided how we are going to respond before listening to everything being said?
- Do we give ourselves the chance to fully understand another point of view by listening properly?
- Do we sometimes dismiss what others say (particularly children) because we consider them of inferior intellect?
- When we listen to other people are we considering how they are feeling when speaking?
- Do we really care what other people have to say?

Social

- Do we shy away from meeting new people?
- Do we regard meeting new people as an interesting opportunity?
- Do we tend to stick with the people we know?
- Are we happy to break away from those we know and meet other people?
- Do we show a genuine interest in others?
- Do we ask interested but unintrusive questions of others?
- Do we remember peoples' names?

Business

- Have we decided the value of a workmate's comments before properly listening to them?
- Do we view each new piece of communication as an opportunity for development?
- Are we sensitive to the feelings and concerns of those we work with?
- Do we take the trouble to find out about our colleagues' families?
- Do we take the trouble to find out what our colleagues' hobbies are?
- Are we genuinely interested in our colleagues' lives outside work?
- Do we think of how we can assist our colleagues in their work?
- Do we take the time to spend a few minutes each day in informal chat?
- Do we really care about our colleagues' well-being?

Domestic

- Have we become too wrapped up in our own working lives to connect properly with our families?
- Do we give value to what our children have to say?
- Do we enquire about our partner's day first?
- Do we focus on what our partner has to say rather than looking for an opportunity to turn the conversation to ourselves?
- Do we take the time to find out what our children have been doing at school?
- Do we know the names of our children's friends and the names of their teachers?

I hear what you are saying

Getting the right emotional status is about being empathetic. Empathy is about listening. Listening is about hearing what someone has to say, being interested in what they have said and remembering what they have said. It is no good just to give the impression of listening – what happens the next time you meet that person and you cannot remember a word they told you before?

If we want to be liked and communicate effectively we must listen, respond and remember. Great salespeople will absorb information about their clients that some people would consider irrelevant, but the next time they meet a client and ask how their daughter's wedding went or if they had a good holiday in Spain, they will be more likely to get the order than the person who has not digested that information. It's a personal touch and we all respond positively to someone who has taken an interest in us.

What's his name?

Charismatic communicators are almost always brilliant at remembering people's names. It is very flattering when someone remembers who you are, and it can inspire great respect for those who do the remembering. It is also extremely tiresome when someone never remembers your name – in fact, you are likely to feel insulted and probably likely to avoid contact with that person in order not to let the situation connect with the extremes of your emotions.

When working on status with one particular client from a rather enormous organization, he related a story about when he was a young and lowly clerk working with a guy who later went on to make the top. Several years later he saw the man again at a company function and congratulated him on his success within the company. Our client was most impressed that the man not only remembered him, his name and where he was working, but took time to indulge in some idle chitchat about how he was getting on and how his family were.

There is no doubt that emotional status and empathy are great contributors to the concept of communicating with charisma.

20
Mental status

The brain is a wonderful organ. It starts working the moment you get up in the morning, and does not stop until you get into the office.

Robert Frost

The brain is indeed a wonderful organ, but it can sometimes take us in directions we should avoid. We need to be in the best frame of mind all day, every day if possible. It's not easy to be upbeat all the time – there are bound to be times when problems play on our minds and hold us back; it's only natural. Adopting the elements that make up great communication should help us discover a mental status that will help us through difficult times and situations. The different areas of status we talk about in this book need to work together for maximum effect, and having the right level of mental status is a key component in this process.

In the theatre, if things do not work well on stage it is all too often down to a lack of attention to the status level of the characters in the play. Well, we are sure that the same can be said for how things work out for all of us in life. We need to be sure that we are applying the right level of status in every area of our performance for complete success. Getting our physical and vocal status right means being in a positive frame of mind, and keeping in check extremes of emotional status. That way every bit of our performance engine can connect properly and run smoothly. The right mental status is the one that acknowledges the need to constantly monitor the other areas to make sure that we are getting the maximum performance from our status levels all the time. It's about being aware.

Beam me up Scottie!

There is one major concern that our calm and rational mental status must address when it comes to giving a good performance: anxiety.

'I hate this – let's get it over with as quickly as possible and get out of here.'

'These people aren't interested in what I'm saying, so let's blast through it and go home.'

'The sooner I can get through this the better, then I can relax.'

Any of these sound familiar? Anxiety when speaking in public is a subject that must be addressed, as more and more of us have to make presentations as part of our working lives. So many of us are thrilled to get the job we want, alas, all too often without realizing that somewhere down the road, standing up and making presentations is going to be a major part of the job. So, the choices are to spend a miserable life finding ways of avoiding it, to look for another job, or to tackle anxiety. Most people are much better at standing up and speaking than they give themselves credit for, but this does nothing to reduce their anxiety.

Some of the people that work for The Speechworks are professional actors who, perversely, put themselves through this kind of agony by choice and are used to being sick into fire buckets before going on stage. Naturally you would expect them to have some techniques and strategies for dealing with the world's number one fear. So, before rushing off for hypnotherapy or seeking the services of a specialist psychologist, let us make a few suggestions.

- Always remember that the audience's wellbeing is the most important thing. The last thing an audience wants is to be nervous on behalf of the person speaking. They want to enjoy themselves. They are more important than you. They need to feel at ease. Your concerns should be for them, not you. They want you to be good. It's not about you – it's about them, what they want and what they want to take away.

- Feeling the part is very important. When actors step out on stage they are in costume. Their costume is an aid to their characterization – it is an integral part of their performance. Get a costume! Including shoes! Take someone with you! Don't step up there wearing what you had on yesterday – this is a special performance. Look good. Treat yourself to something you wouldn't normally wear to work. Get a new aftershave or perfume. Feel the part.

- When the curtain rises on a play the actors are already in character. They have been warming up and preparing for the last 30/60 minutes. Start your performance early. When you have read this book and you understand the components that make up charisma, put them together well before you stand up to speak. Be in character when you leave the house or when you walk through the doors at work in the morning. Start your performance early, and when you begin your presentation you will already be halfway through the show.

- You are the expert. You are being asked to speak because you know your subject. What you have to offer your audience is gold dust. If you believe in your material it will support you. Have faith in your material and remember why it is you standing up there speaking – you are the expert!

- Try to embrace the artificiality of the situation. This is not an occasion where you are having an informal chat to a small group of people around a table in a bar. An audience always enjoys these unnatural situations. Perhaps we should recognize that that is what they are and accept them for that. Help the audience to enjoy the artificiality even more. Play the part.

It is an irrefutable fact that the best cure for anxiety when speaking in public is to be thoroughly prepared. It means bringing the three principal components of great communication into play: Story, Status and Focus. We know that audiences enjoy the combination of SSF. We know that they work! A little dedication to the areas of Story, Status and Focus will have a positive impact on developing your charisma. Just those three things! Nothing more.

Be the best

We owe it to ourselves to be as good as we possibly can, and we can be good if we take the time to digest and employ SSF. We can send our audience home saying 'Wow! That was good!' Being in that positive mental state to bring SSF together and get it working for us will have the desired effect. There is nothing quite as empowering as knowing that you have a good game and are a match for anyone in your own way.

21

Status in business

I believe in businesses where you engage in creative thinking, and where you form some of your deepest relationships. If it isn't about the production of the human spirit, we are in big trouble.

Anita Roddick

If we are going to function with maximum effect in our working lives we need to have that open and neutral status that lets others in. If we close ourselves down with a status that is too low or too high then we'll be denying those we do business with access to ourselves, thus making any meaningful communication impossible. So many people make the mistake of adopting a level of status that they believe is in line with their position. In fact, for some, it is the excuse they have been looking for to 'Lord it' over their subordinates.

Wrong! As we said before the kind of status we are talking about in this book has nothing to do with position or hierarchy, it is about how we are perceived regardless of title or position in the pecking order.

Be afraid – be very afraid!

We must stay on the lookout for anyone who uses their position to flex their muscles and assumes their status is higher than those around them. If we look at the aggressively high status man at the beginning of the book we will find a person whose status actually gets in the way of productive work. He believes that he will get the best out of people by shouting at them and keeping them in a constant state of fear. What a fool! The reverse is actually true. Those working under this person will be more prone to make mistakes, and will then try to cover up their errors and sweep them under the carpet. It will only be a matter of time before King Kong looks underneath the carpet and explodes. This person may well be very clever and have a great knowledge of his subject, but by using the wrong level of status his people skills will be zero and his department's productivity nil.

What's your handicap?

We once worked with a man who would boast about the dressing-downs he dished out to his workforce, and firmly believed that these tongue-lashings were having a positive effect. He also enjoyed telling stories about putting people down and scoring points over those around him. He was a keen golfer and one of these stories was about a member of his staff who tried to curry favour by suggesting they had a round of golf together. This is how our man responded:

'Look, Ken – you play off twenty-four, I play off six – you're going to lose a lot of balls and I'm not. You're going to feel bad when you're in the trees trying to get on the fairway and I'm going to get frustrated with you. I do not want a six-hour round of golf thank you. Maybe in a couple of years' time when you've stopped hacking round. OK?'

He told this story almost as if he was being cruel to be kind, but the subtext was, how good he was at putting people in their place. Not only was the level of status wrong – he could not see that he had missed a golden opportunity. A boss with the right level of status and the right understanding of the needs of his staff would have accepted the invitation, and looked on a quick nine holes as a way of getting to know the man better and even helping him with some useful tips about his swing.

What was his handicap? His inability to communicate properly.

The third man

One of our colleagues came up with an interesting theory about people who play high status. She was working with a senior business figure from a major UK company who could never be wrong. This person was usually late for a session, but would never be able to apologize. On one occasion when arriving 30 minutes late he spoke about himself in the third person and rather grandly announced:

'He's arrived!'

Extraordinary behaviour! Her observation and conclusion as to why this person behaved in that way was that high status people can be afraid that they won't be liked if they reveal themselves. This, of course, demonstrates a fundamental weakness. When dealing with high status people in our business lives we must always remember this. Claiming status over others will make us look insecure.

People who wish to establish a higher status than others will never be at an advantage. We must never assume that our status is higher than others. We must never assume that we are better or worse than others. We must always recognize the worth of others without backing down or fronting up, and only a middle level of status can achieve this – the charisma level.

They all hate me!

Dangerous levels of high status are always the most apparent in a business environment. People often make the huge mistake of associating success with high status. They couldn't be more wrong. Yes, some people achieve success in their business lives by adopting unreasonably high levels of status and thus incur low levels of popularity. They most likely won't even be aware of, or, quite possibly, even care about their unpopularity. When a person succeeds in making themselves unpopular they have failed. They have made a bad choice. They have poisoned the atmosphere and are unlikely to get the best out of colleagues – both junior and, surprisingly, senior. By opting for the middle ground they might have been even more successful and certainly more popular. What is the point of saying, 'Look at what I have achieved!' if nobody likes you?

There are, of course, those who get a perverse kind of pleasure out of not being liked because they believe that if they are feared that will give them power. We think that's a rather twisted outlook. Great communicators do not rule by fear. Great communicators manage their business successfully because they have learned to listen, they have learned to be aware, they have learned to understand the views and values of those around them and they have only been able to do this by assuming the right level of status. The extremes are as bad as each other – only the middle ground will do.

The interview

When attending job interviews we have all had bad experiences at the hands of our interviewers because of their appalling choice of status. Let's look at three different scenarios of being greeted for the first time.

● The interviewer remains behind their desk, half rises to shake hands, just about manages to look at you though their eyebrows and mumbles some sort of greeting.

● The interviewer remains seated behind their desk, orders you to take a seat and gestures towards the chair opposite without looking up.

● The interviewer comes out of their room to collect you, shakes you warmly by the hand, introduces themselves and asks how your journey was.

In the first case, by demonstrating low status characteristics, the interviewer has virtually shut down any meaningful communication and has probably stopped you from having any respect for them. In the second case, through high status behaviour, the interviewer has closed off proper communication and has probably either intimidated you or just annoyed you. The third interviewer has done everything right by going for the middle ground and has brought about the right conditions for good communication. It's not difficult and the benefits are great.

The first two interviewers immediately threw up barriers that were going to be difficult, if not impossible, to overcome. What madness! The third interviewer seemed pleased to meet you and by greeting you outside the room, put you at ease in their environment. They then showed an interest in how you got to them by striking up cordial conversation and again putting you at ease. What they did was to create a situation where they are going to get the very best out of you and not miss the opportunity that you could be great for their company: 5–7 every time. It's a no-brainer!

Who will buy?

Let's look at another business situation – sales. Never was there a more important area for getting the level of status absolutely bang on. If we do not use the right level of status in sales we stand little or no chance of ever selling anything. There might be a remote possibility that the low status salesperson will get an order because the buyer feels sorry for them, but that will be a one-off. There could be a slim chance that a high status salesperson might make a sale through intimidation, but repeat business is unlikely. No, the best way to succeed in sales is through the charming band of status (5–7) – open, accessible, warm and non-threatening.

Sales is not about selling. Anyone who thinks that they are going to go out there and sell to people is barking up the wrong tree. People do not like being sold to. Successful sales can only be achieved by building relationships, and that is not achievable for low and high status people. Low and high status salespeople are not capable of forging long-term, meaningful relationships with clients.

A client has to feel that they can trust a salesperson. A client must not feel that they are having something pushed at them, that they neither want nor need. Only an open and neutral status can be successful in sales. Buyers need to operate in the comfort of a situation in which they are not going to be hit by the hard sell. They want to be in a situation where their supplier is a friend and adviser, not someone who wants to fill up the order book as quickly as possible.

The lower status salesperson is unlikely to operate the hard sell, but the high status salesperson may well do so. Middle ground status in sales is where business can flourish with no one feeling pressured to buy or make a sale. It's so simple and it works! People in sales generally tend to be in the middle to high level of status bracket, but it is the middle level that will be more successful. Anyone who adopts the charisma level of status in their life in sales will enjoy long-lasting and fruitful relationships with their clients.

The relationship

Successful middle ground status in sales is about being there for your clients at all times – not just when you want an order or a contract. Being there for our clients regardless of financial gain is important. It's about giving, not taking. Middle status people are givers and it's givers who get. Low and high status take. They can bleed a person dry, and that's no way to operate in business. It is the low key offering of help, guidance and expertise that will always pay dividends. If you want something from somebody, be prepared to give something of yourself.

The one-day experiment

This is something we should all do on a regular basis. The next time you go into work, analyse every single piece of communication you have. Think very carefully about how you address and interact with everyone you come into contact with, from the caretaker to the chairman of the board.

- Did you acknowledge the person who runs the car park?

- Did you say good morning to the person who sold you your train ticket?

- Did you say hello to the person on reception, or did you walk straight past?

- Did you ask your PA about his/her weekend?

- Did you speak to the person at the next desk or in the next office and find out how they are?

- Did you make a list of people you need to contact today?

- Did you make a list of these you don't need to contact but it might be good if you did?

- Did you ask the person who serves you your lunch how they are?

- Did you think about each piece of communication beforehand to make sure that you approached it in a positive way?

It really doesn't take a lot to do any of this, but the benefits could be huge and the good feeling that you create will spread through the building. Imagine what might happen if everyone did the one-day experiment – a happy working environment. Imagine what might happen if everyone did the one-day experiment every day – the company's productivity would almost certainly increase. Remember: 5–7 every time.

22

Status on stage

Acting is all about honesty. If you can fake that you've got it made.

Attributed to George Burns

Status on stage is a bit like status in life. Acting is, after all, art reflecting life. Status on stage has a very broad spectrum. Understanding the extremes of status is very important when finding the charisma level of status. Theatre is probably the finest medium in which to demonstrate the extremes of status.

It is an actor's job to explore status, to keep an eye out for its subtle changes and react accordingly. During their careers actors will have discovered and hopefully played every level of status to be found in the theatre. This is what makes the job of the actor fascinating. If an actor is unaware of status and its varying degrees then they will not succeed in their work. The success of every piece of theatre is dependent on the fluctuation of the status of the characters in the play. Every time a new character appears on stage, the status of the characters already in the space should shift if only slightly to accommodate the new person on stage – if this does not happen, there is something wrong with the production.

Is it working?

Examining status on stage is a wonderful way of gauging if a production is on the right track. Actors, directors and writers are all well advised to pay special attention to where the status of their characters is at every point in the play. If something doesn't feel right, look right, sound right, or if the play just isn't working for some reason, check the status of the characters and if they are being correctly affected by the other characters in the piece. This usually sorts things out!

The shifting plates of theatre

The most powerful and dramatic pieces of theatre are when massive shifts of status occur. When kings are deposed or when even stranger things are at play, as in the case of Richard II who deliberately reduced his status to martyrdom by his abdication. There are wonderful swinging changes of status throughout Shakespeare's *Julius Caesar*. A man's status is reduced to nothing when a powerful nobleman is wrongfully incarcerated, as in *The Count of Monte Cristo* who creates yet another massive status shift on his return to society. Great examples of the ever-moving plates of status can be found in more contemporary pieces of theatre, such as Noel Coward's *Hay Fever* or *The Sea* by Edward Bond. It is when such great changes of status happen that an audience gasps and we know that the play is working well.

It is useful for us to remember and remind ourselves about these dramatic changes of status on stage. When we observe the pendulum of status it becomes absolutely apparent how damaging the extremes can be. We may feel that the damage we see in the theatre has no bearing on our own lives in the real world but we'd be wrong. We will all, at some stage, be subject to someone using extremes of status for their own gain and it will be, at the least, unpleasant.

It can be manipulative and used for self-preservation at the expense of others. It might also reflect a lack of self-confidence which is highly evident in the blustering bully. The more we understand about status and its extremes, and the more we are aware of it, the less damage we will suffer.

The more soundly based we are in our middle status, the better equipped we will be to counteract the assault of extreme status. Abusers of extreme status in plays invariably get their come-uppance – the same is largely true in life. If we think about the abusive despots throughout history, it is reasonably true to say that they have almost all met a sticky end. If you take high status it is there to be taken away. If you adopt manipulative low status – you will eventually be rumbled. No one can reasonably take exception to an open and neutral status.

Once more unto the breach

Earlier in this book we alluded to Shakespeare's *Henry V* as an illustration of great emotional investment. It is also one of the best examples of the success of mid-level status on stage. If you do not have time to read the play or to go the theatre to see it, go online to YouTube and take a look at Henry V's Saint Crispin's Day speech as performed by Laurence Olivier and Kenneth Branagh. The same words delivered in completely different ways, but with the same level of status.

The story is that Henry's army, which is made up of the soldiers of noblemen loyal to him, are battle-weary and vastly outnumbered when they encounter the might of the French army at Agincourt. The speech takes place minutes before both armies engage in combat. It is a heartfelt, motivational speech of thanks that inspires the English soldiers to victory. The adoption of mid-level status in both performances is so moving that many would wish themselves there to take up arms. Historians will tell us that the noblemen of England who fought that day did not follow Henry because he ordered them to (in fact, Henry had to humbly ask for their help) nor did they take part because they felt sorry for him. They were there for him because of his great leadership through mid-level status – his charisma.

The next time you are in the theatre, pay special attention to the status levels of the characters and see how they change and develop throughout the play. If there is no shift of status when a new character enters, then you are watching a poor piece of theatre. If there is a constant fluctuation of status levels in the piece, the director and the actors are doing their jobs properly. The actors will be 'mirroring life'. They may be doing this in a somewhat dramatic way – but they are, nevertheless, reflecting reality by their fine observation of character status.

When you next visit the cinema do the same. A good piece of film-making will have the necessary shifts of status. If it does not it is an inferior production.

Actors on screen will use status in the same way that actors on stage do. It may be done a little more subtly, a flick of the eye, a slight adjustment of posture or a tiny change of voice pitch. The only difference between the shifts of status in theatre and life is that the former may be heightened for dramatic effect – otherwise they are exactly the same. Observing status levels and their effects on stage and film is a great way of identifying and understanding how status works, and it's safer than doing it in public and running the risk of upsetting someone in real life by staring at them.

'I love acting. It is so much more real than life.' Oscar Wilde, of course.

23
Status in life

Happiness is when what you think, what you say and what you do are in harmony.

Mohandas (Mahatma) Gandhi

It may seem a little corny, but Gandhi got it right. Bringing all the aspects of mid-level status together is the perfect recipe for achieving the very best we can in every area of our lives. It may take a little effort but the rewards will be great. We have seen what can be done with mid-level status in our business lives and when performing – now we need to apply the same principles to our lives in general.

By now there should be absolutely no argument that the 5–7 channel is where we need to be – the area where charisma is most effective. Let's think back to that rather idealistic notion we spoke about earlier in this book where everyone woke up one morning with mid-level status, and what a wonderful world that would create. OK, it's not going to happen in a global sense, but we can make it happen in our own worlds. We can have a positive effect on those around us and see how great the ripple effect might be. There can be no doubt that other people will feel the benefit of our mid-level status and that, in turn, will make us feel good too. A circle of positive feedback!

Stephen Fry, no less, has noted that, 'It's very hard to be happy if you're not good and it's very easy to be good if you're happy.'

We can all have that marvellously empowering feeling that mid-level status brings. That confidence in the knowledge that we have equipped ourselves to deal with any difficult situation with our strength in mid-level status. The happiness we can get from getting the best out of the important people in our lives. The satisfaction we can achieve by creating win-win situations.

The leader

Personal power is stronger than positional power, true, but personal power is key for those who wish to obtain positional power. The great leaders throughout history have all possessed immense personal power or charisma. Churchill, Roosevelt, Gandhi, Mandela, Kennedy, Clinton – every one of them equipped with the skills of inspiring and motivating. These people are not unique in their qualities; they have simply recognized their skills and used them to communicate their vision to others.

In return, those around them bring creativity and commitment to their work. They feel empowered by their leader's confidence in them and are gratified by their approval. The charismatic qualities of these leaders draw people around them into an emotional bond. They feel valued and worthy. They are infected with their leader's zest and passion and are happy to do their bidding. This is the power of the charismatic leader. They are an indomitable force that fires the imagination and intelligence of those around them. They build trust and make dreams tangible. They use their energy to generate excitement and enthusiasm. They are people who have changed the course of history through their personalities.

Have you got it?

Yes you have! We can all be more appealing than we already are, and it's largely about status. Genuine mid-level status is the way to go. Low status will not command respect – high status will have an initial shock impact but will ultimately close us down. Charismatic people appear open and strong, and genuine mid-level status will provide an undeniable strength that we find appealing.

Part
05

Communicating with charisma – Story, Status, Focus

All I want to see from an actor is the intensity and accuracy of their listening.

Alan Rickman

Next in importance to having a good aim is to recognize when to pull the trigger.

David Letterman

24

The attraction of focus

Focus on the other actors as if they were the most important characters in the play – mind you if the scene is yours – grab it!

John Hurt

We all understand the importance of being focused but what does it actually mean and how can it improve our performance? Focus and concentration are major contributors to our success in life. If we do not focus and concentrate on the things that are important to us we are sure to fail. Whether we are studying for an exam, working on a report or creating a presentation, focus and concentration are paramount.

They are particularly important when we are 'performing'. We must be focused from the moment we enter the performing area to the moment we leave it. If we are not focused we will lose our audience and stand little or no chance of managing their focus. Once we have decided what we are going to say and have adopted the right status for the job, it is time to apply focus to our delivery. Focus will play a major role in developing your charisma.

Enjoy the show Mrs Lincoln?

Watching the best actors deliver their lines is an object lesson in the effective management of focus. Whether it is on stage or on film, the skill of successfully directing focus is a pre-required ability for all actors – without it their performances will count for nothing. When we watch a good piece of theatre or film our focus and attention will move seamlessly between the characters on stage – this is because the actors are doing their job properly. With their own focus and concentration, they are steering our attention to where it needs to be for the piece to make sense. If an actor is only concerned with their own performance and not the piece as a whole, they will pull focus and divert our attention from where it should be. Some actors pull focus by visibly reacting to everything that is said without actually listening – these people shouldn't be allowed near a stage or a camera and should possibly be shot.

25

The focus puller

Do not dwell in the past, do not dream of the future, concentrate the mind on the present moment.

Gautama Buddha

In the film industry the focus puller has the extremely important job of managing the focus of the camera and measuring the shot.

In life, the focus puller has a very negative connotation. He or she will always 'grab it' whether it is theirs to grab or not and we all know who they are. They are in every walk of life. They are at work, they are probably in your family and even among the people you socialize with. They will dominate; they care little or nothing for others. They are attention seekers who will do anything to snatch the focus in any situation – 'me me me me'.

Gail Blanke says get rid of 50 things – make the focus puller one of them!

Now's the time

As Buddha said, actors must live in the *now*. It is essential that all performers are performing in the present and not getting ahead of themselves. They need to know their material so well that they do not have to think ahead and can focus on the now. This is often a problem with focus pullers who have already decided how they are going to react (whether it is necessary to do so or not), get ahead of themselves and telegraph what's coming. Atrocious!

It's not just bad actors that get ahead of themselves. A great many people who have to stand and deliver are guilty of not living in the now when they perform, and this is not because they are self-centred like the hams on stage. It can be for a number of non-egocentric reasons. It might be because they have a very quick mind and they are already thinking ahead to the next page of their presentation rather than staying with the moment. It may be because they would rather be anywhere else, and that the sooner they finish the better they will feel. Either way they are doing themselves a great disservice and are short-changing their audience. We need to stop and think what we are doing. Racing through a presentation or any form of communication will destroy the focus of an audience and it will not make us feel any better. We must deliver three times more slowly than we would read in our head. Living and performing in the now will hold an audience's attention and give the speaker more satisfaction as a result. Let's start living in the now and give our charisma a chance to shine through.

Please note that although we are talking about presentation in this section of the book, focus techniques apply to all forms of communication.

Easy does it

When we are being trained in presentation or public speaking skills, we will almost always be told to slow down; but we also need to understand *why* we are galloping through our material, and with that understanding focus on the needs of our audience. When we have done that and are performing in the *now* we will have taken an enormous step towards improving our delivery and pleasing our audience. It's very easy to understand the logic behind being in the now but it is perhaps even easier to drift back into giving a breakneck paced delivery. Let's live and focus in the now.

All the great communicators are Grand Masters when it comes to focus. Every moment for them is a now moment. What is most important to them is what they are saying at that particular moment and the effect it is having on those who are listening to them at that moment. What is important to them is that they have the full attention of their audience and that they have not lost them by racing ahead. Great communicators understand the power of focus and use it with tremendous effect.

What do we need to do?

So, let's assume that we are starting to pay greater attention to the importance of focus and concentration. How do we build on that? How do we enhance our performance with the power of focus? Well, in the way that actors are able to guide the focus of their audience around the stage in order for them to follow the story, presenting in public is much the same. The only big difference is the abolition of the 'fourth wall'.

The fourth wall in theatre is the invisible wall that separates the audience from the stage. Only when performing in pantomime or delivering asides in restoration comedy or melodrama will an actor speak directly to an audience. A presenter speaks directly to an audience all the time. Rather than steering an audience's focus through the story of a play, the speaker has to use focus to guide their audience through the story of their presentation or speech. If you agreed with what we said at the beginning of this book you will know that every piece of communication is, in fact, a story.

26

Stanislavski – the father of focus and godfather of method acting

To grasp the full significance of life is the actor's duty, to interpret it is his problem, and to express it his dedication.

Marlon Brando

Stan's the man

When actors train they will almost certainly study the teachings of Konstantin Stanislavski, the man who created the first 'system' of acting. Stanislavski paid particular attention to focus and concentration. He believed that an audience's focus could be managed by using the *three circles of concentration*, or *circles of attention*. Let's call them the circles of concentration.

There are many different styles of presenting and there is no hard and fast rule as to which is right. There is, however, one method that really does need to be avoided. We have all witnessed the speaker who buries their face in their notes. The speaker who does not look up from their notes. The speaker who is simply reading to us. This kind of presentation does not really connect with an audience. If we are just going to look down and read what is on the paper we will not be able to use the circles of concentration and we will definitely not be able to manage the focus of our audience. It is possible to use both notes and the circles, but the speaker must be able to lift the message off the page and deliver it out front.

Konstantin Stanislavski (1863–1938)

Stanislavski was born Konstantin Sergeyevich Alekseyev in Moscow in the time of tsarist Russia and Peter the Great. His father was a wealthy merchant who had made his fortune manufacturing gold and silver thread.

Interested in theatre from an early age, Konstantin took the stage name Stanislavski when 25 and set up the Moscow Society of Art and Literature. In 1898 he co-founded the Moscow Art Theatre – the first ensemble theatre in Russia.

At the Moscow Art Theatre Stanislavski started to develop his own system of training actors, which would help them achieve a more realistic and believable style of acting. He challenged the traditional ideas of those times about drama and performance, and went on to pioneer a more naturalist school of thought. He used his system to bring the works of such playwrights as Chekhov and Gorky to life.

Chekhov and Stanislavski's collaboration at Moscow Art Theatre resulted in the realization of the Chekhovian stage classics *The Seagull*, *Uncle Vanya*, *The Three Sisters* and *The Cherry Orchard*. Stanislavski also starred in several classical plays as an actor himself. His performances as Othello, and as Gayev in *The Cherry Orchard* were highly acclaimed both by critics and the public.

His process of character development, the 'Stanislavski Method', was the catalyst for the development of method acting, or 'The Method' as it is known. It is said by many to be the most influential acting system ever developed. It was first popularized by the Group Theatre in New York in the 1930s, and then advanced by Lee Strasberg at The Actors Studio in the 1940s and 1950s. The Actors Studio is run today as a non-profit organization for professional actors, directors and playwrights.

The Stanislavski system is still the basis of a large part of actor training and practice. His methods and theories are still read today in his books, including *My Life in Art* (1924), *An Actor Prepares* (1926), and *Building a Character* (1950).

His house in central Moscow is now a public museum dedicated to his life.

Stanislavski wanted to find an approach to acting that would be of benefit to all actors, but he himself famously said of his own system:

'Create your own method. Don't depend slavishly on mine. Make up something that will work for you. But keep breaking traditions I beg you.'

The godfather of method acting

How does an actor act? That was the question Stanislavski dedicated his life to exploring. His work proved to be an enormous contribution to twentieth-century theatre and film. His legacy lives on today. Just some of the actors who are said to have been influenced by Stanislavski and his system include Jack Nicholson, Al Pacino, Robert de Niro, Kevin Spacey, Marlon Brando, James Dean, Johnny Depp, Russell Crowe, Leonardo DiCaprio, Denzel Washington, Anthony Hopkins, Judi Dench, Sean Penn, Dustin Hoffman, Steve McQueen, Paul Newman, Warren Beatty, Harvey Keitel, Jane Fonda, and many more. Indeed, some directors would say that Stanislavski has had an influence on every good actor in the world.

Be prepared

Mark Twain said: 'It usually takes more than three weeks to prepare a good impromptu speech.'

But seriously.

In order for Stanislavski's circles to be at their most effective, a presentation or keynote speech must be properly prepared and the speaker needs to be more than familiar with the material – then focus and concentration can add colour and texture to the presentation, turning it into a compelling performance. You will, no doubt, have been told that there is no substitute for good preparation. This is, of course, true and if we are to move to a higher level of performance, good preparation and familiarization is essential.

The three circles of concentration

Let's assume that we have done our homework and prepared well. We have washed down the walls, rolled on the emulsion, we have sanded the woodwork and put on the undercoat – time to apply the gloss. We have a good story that is constructed well, that travels with fluidity, that is brutally edited yet is alive with spontaneity. We have adopted the perfect middle ground status that makes us strong and accessible. Time to bring the circles into play and really get that charisma working!

We like to describe the three circles of concentration in filmic terms:

Third circle – the master shot

Second circle – the intimate 2 shot

First circle – the single close-up

'What on earth does that mean?' we hear you scream! Let's break things down in the next chapter.

27

Countdown to charisma – the three circles of concentration

A great actor is independent of the poet, because the supreme essence of feeling does not reside in prose or in verse, but in the accent with which it is delivered.

Lee Strasberg

Third circle

The establishing or master shot

The shot that sets the scene. Imagine you are a film director. There you are, seated in your wood and canvas chair with your name on the back, looking like Steven Spielberg. The clapperboard reveals the name of the movie 'Focus – this time it's personal!' The first thing you need to do is to create a platform to work from – a solid base. One shot that could, if necessary, tell the story of the scene. This is what is known in the business as the master shot – the safety shot. It's a shot that can be cut back to in order to re-establish where we are in the plot. It's our failsafe. There is little or no point in progressing any further with our movie until we are happy with our master shot – it is the very foundation, and without that continuity we do not have a film.

How does this relate to our presentations and speeches? Well, in much the same way that a film-maker requires a platform to work from, so do we as speakers. We need our own master shot – our safety shot that we can return to when we need to establish our relationship with our audience. The only difference being, that as speakers we never leave our third circle of concentration. We are constantly in third. From our third circle of concentration we are able to engage second and first which will we come to later. We will be able to cut into our master shot to create our own 'presentation movie'.

The energy of the third circle

Our third circle is the energy with which we engage our audience. We need to be able think a little abstractly here. We all generate an energy when we stand up to speak – some more than others. This is something that we need to be very aware of. This is something that we can control. This is an energy that most of us will need to increase. This energy takes in our whole audience – it embraces everyone in the working space and we must maintain the optimum level of third circle energy at all times. When we have acquired a high level of third circle energy we will be well on the way to completing the charisma puzzle.

Use the force

A few years ago we were invited by a client to join them for an event at the O$_2$ Arena in London where Bill Clinton was speaking. Meeting the former President was no disappointment – this is a man who does exactly what it says on the tin! Without wishing to sound sycophantic, when Bill Clinton entered the room it was as if someone had flipped the 'on' switch to a whole new bank of lights – a new and effective energy had entered the room. This was a man who had no problem inhabiting that third circle of concentration and maintaining its energy. Later when he was introduced on stage to speak it was abundantly clear that he was still very much in that third circle. He calmly entered on stage, took in the audience with a smile as he approached the podium, carefully arranged his notes, slowly removed his glasses case from his inside pocket, equally slowly removed his glasses from the case and put them on, looked up and engaged his audience once again. This process probably took around about a minute and at no time were we allowed to escape the Clinton third circle of concentration. He had us!

What is this energy force thing? This third circle stuff probably sounds a bit weird. Maybe it is a bit weird, but what we have to do is connect with those on the perimeter of our audience. In a conventional theatre-style presentation we must consciously think about including the people on the sides of the auditorium and those at the very back, which can sometimes call for a bigger performance than we might be comfortable with. Don't worry – it may feel a little strange or even over the top, but it will not appear like that to our audience. In truth, they will think more of us for including everyone in our address – and not just those in the first few rows.

Here's another little abstract thought to wrestle with – by sending out our energy of third circle to the outer reaches of our audience, our energy and attention will automatically fall on those people inside the perimeter of our audience – nobody will feel left out. Third circle energy neglects no one.

Third circle is the focal starting point for any form of public address. When in doubt, include everyone – get the message to the back and the sides – if we do that, those in the middle will automatically be taken care of. The safety shot. Presentational skills trainers will always tell you that you must project your voice to the back of the space so everyone can hear you – well, yes, but you could look down at the floor and be heard at the back – so it's a little bit more than that and that is why we talk about energy. Physical, vocal and emotional energy are needed in equal quantities to sustain third circle focus. And remember, we never leave our third circle of concentration. Hopefully third circle is starting to feel a little less weird. Third circle – our focus base.

When story and status are working well we can use focus to colour our performance, and third circle is the foundation of that focus. What Bill Clinton did with his third circle of concentration at the O_2 Arena we are all capable of doing. Once we acknowledge the effect that third circle energy can have on an audience, we can work to apply it.

When presenting to a large audience, third circle is probably the most important of the three. Certainly, when working in a large space one can almost scrape by without using second and first if necessary. The next time you are at the theatre, pay special attention to see if the actors are using their third circle with good effect. If you are watching a quality piece of theatre the actors will certainly be maximizing the impact of their third circle of concentration to connect with the audience through the fourth wall. They may not be addressing the audience directly but they will be using their third circle energy to engage them.

When the focus base of third circle is working well, a good presenter can slip in and out of second and first whilst remaining in third to give a variety of focus. This is where the circles of concentration come into their own. This is where a speaker who has embraced the value of the circles can switch, steer and hold an audience's focus. If a speaker loses focus, their audience will cease to be engaged and entertained. So how do we move from pure third to second in third?

Second circle

The window to the soul

Second circle – the intimate two shot. We might call it the intimate two shot but we are of course concentrating on the focus of one person – the speaker – who in turn will distribute their own focus between individuals or groups of people.

Anyone who has had any form of presentation skills training will have been told:

'You've got to have eye contact, you know.'

Well, yes that is true, but what does it mean, and why, and how long for? We'll deal with that in a moment, but first why is eye contact so important? It's important because it means that we are connecting with people. We are paying attention to others. We are showing an interest in those around us, and that doesn't just mean the people we are addressing in a presentation. It's important that we have eye contact with those we are engaging with, no matter what the situation. Whether we are having a casual conversation at work, whether we are being introduced to someone new, or whether we are giving a report to the boss we have to look them in the eye – it shows respect. It also helps us to gauge their reaction to what we are saying and allows them to do the same.

'Find your mark, look the other fellow in the eye and tell the truth' comes from James Cagney.

It's all very well being told that we must have eye contact with our audience, but what if we are addressing over 100 people? Can we possibly have eye contact with everyone? Of course not – but through our random selection of those we do make eye contact with, we can give the impression that we are personally addressing everyone.

Still lookin'?

'You lookin' at me?' enquired Robert de Niro in the film *Taxi Driver.*

How long for?

In a one-to-one conversation we might hold eye contact all the way through – it's a matter of being sensitive to how the other person feels about it. When addressing an audience – two to three seconds tops! If we look at one person out of an audience of 200 people for too long that person is going to feel very uncomfortable, and the other 199 will feel ignored and left out. It is important to shift our second circle of concentration frequently. This is what great communicators do and that is what makes their audiences feel personally addressed, even though they haven't managed to take them all in individually.

In the limelight

TV news readers and presenters have a natural choice of focus with second circle, and they engage with us almost entirely through that circle alone – even though they are subconsciously still in third.

Actors can use second circle of concentration with great dramatic effect. As John Hurt indicated in his 'grab it' advice we quoted earlier – second circle is a wonderful tool to centre the focus on other people, and it can also be used to reverse that focus back on to ourselves. Let's take a look at some classic examples of great second circles of concentration from the movies.

Absent fish

It is probably safe to say that everyone has seen *Jaws*. There is a marvellous scene midway through the film where Robert Shaw, Richard Dreyfus and Roy Scheider are at sea at night drinking below decks. Shaw tells the story of his ship being torpedoed in the South Atlantic during the war. The men were helpless in the icy water and were slowly being picked off by the sharks. During this story Shaw ignores Dreyfus and focuses on Scheider. The story he tells is rather harrowing and lasts for about two minutes. During that period Shaw never takes his eyes off Scheider – he doesn't even appear to blink. This choice of heightened second circle of concentration makes the story especially chilling. His tone is measured, the volume low and the intensity of his focus makes this scene one of the most powerful in the film, without a fish in sight.

Step aside

You may remember a wonderful BBC series called *The House of Cards,* with Ian Richardson playing Sir Francis Urquhart, Chief Whip turned Prime Minister. Writer Andrew Davies used the old restoration style aside to great effect in a modern day context. We all waited with anticipation for the next time when Richardson would use the device to step outside of the action, fix us with his steely blue eyes and deliver a 'little do they know' style quip.

What's my name?

In *Gladiator,* Russell Crowe does a fine job with second circle when he addresses the man who killed his family. Crowe looks the actor firmly in the eye and tells him who he is. In the same way as Shaw's story in *Jaws,* this short scene is one of the film's most memorable moments, and that is almost entirely due to this skilled actor's superb employment of second circle of concentration.

Two's company

When there are two principal characters in a film we know that there will be an abundance of wonderful second circle. Edward Albee's brilliantly crafted psychological battle between Richard Burton and Elizabeth Taylor in *Who's Afraid of Virginia Woolf?* demonstrates the devastating power of the second circle. The interplay between 'dentist' Laurence Olivier and Dustin Hoffman in *Marathon Man* will live long in the memory of cinemagoers everywhere, with both actors treating us to ample helpings of second circle of concentration. Olivier does this equally brilliantly with Michael Caine in *Sleuth.*

Whose baby?

Fatal Attraction is a marvellous film. There is one scene in particular that sends shivers racing down the spine, and it is not the one with the rabbit in the pot! When Glenn Close tells Michael Douglas that she is pregnant and she intends to keep the baby, she works the second circle of concentration brilliantly well, giving Douglas so much to work with. She calmly holds his gaze as he races through a series of disturbing emotions – two actors getting the very best out of the circles of concentration.

Having an old friend for dinner

One of the most disturbing deployments of second circle in the cinema came from Anthony Hopkins in *Silence of the Lambs*. It is a classic example of how great writing can build an actor's part by depriving the audience of access to the character for as long as possible. Consequently when we do meet Hopkins we are not disappointed. The scene begins when Jodie Foster is making her way cell by cell to confront Hopkins, not knowing which cell he is in. At last when we encounter Hopkins standing quite still staring out of his cell, his intense control of second circle of concentration provides one of the most chilling moments in cinema history. None of us will forget the day we met Hannibal Lecter!

Giving the eye

Next time you are told, 'You must have eye contact, you know', remember the second circle of concentration. All of the above are very powerful illustrations of the use of second circle, so let's be careful how we use it. We don't want to be engaging people with a Hannibal Lecter style use of focus, or connecting with a Laurence Olivier drill-wielding manner either. We need to think about the different ways our eye contact can affect other people and make decisions about the kind of impression we want to have on others.

The reason for using our second circle of concentration is generally to connect with people in a positive, friendly, interested and caring way which in itself carries great power and influence. It's a bit more than just having eye contact. Our eyes are very expressive organs – they say a lot about us and are wonderful instruments for conveying feelings and emotions, wishes and desires, likes and dislikes. The window to the soul. So, yes, it is important to have eye contact, but let's understand what that can mean – and no wide-eyed staring – that's just scary!

Get a grip

Engaging with our audience visually will always be the most memorable form of contact, so it is important that we get to grips with all three circles of concentration. With third circle we've acknowledged the bigger picture, and we've seen the power of second circle operating within third. Now we're beginning to piece this focus thing together and pretty soon we will enjoy the benefits of communicating with charisma.

First circle

The single close-up

How many times has someone said to you 'I can hear you thinking' when you have been in a moment of reverie? Plenty, no doubt.

One of things we have agreed on at The Speechworks is that it is absolutely fascinating watching someone think. Whether a person is speaking or not, watching someone internalize information and process thought is very interesting indeed. This is what the single close-up is all about.

The first circle of concentration is the thinking circle. It is the slightly de-focused, introspective circle that acts as a springboard for a new dynamic, a new thought. It is the circle that brings spontaneity to a performance – and let's remember that all the best told stories are told with spontaneity and enthusiasm.

One-to-one

Great communicators make fine use of first circle, particularly when being interviewed. How many times have we seen politicians answer questions almost before they have finished being asked? You will never see skilful interviewees do this. They will allow interviewers to finish their question. They will then retreat into their first circle of concentration – sometimes only momentarily – and then give a reply. They do this even if they do know the answer to the question before the interviewer has finished asking it. The use of first circle in this situation does three things:

- It pays respect to the person who is asking the question.
- It acknowledges value in the question being asked.
- It demonstrates thought and consideration in the response.

Getting the right measurement of first circle is absolutely crucial. Not too little to appear cocksure and not too much to appear self-indulgent. We have all witnessed wrong measures of first circle. Too little can actually get to the point where there is none at all, and the interviewee gives no value to the question or the person asking it. Too much can give the impression that the interviewee thinks that we are hanging on their every word, and are waiting with bated breath for the pearls of wisdom in an over-considered response. First circle must appear genuine.

One for all

We must use first circle of concentration with great care and be most sparing with it. Its use in the interview format is interesting and shows respect. When using first circle in addressing a larger audience we must choose where to apply it very carefully. We have to bear in mind that in this type of presentation we are supposed to know what we are talking about, so over-use of first circle may come across as false and contrived. Careful selection of areas in which to use first circle can be very effective indeed. If we make good decisions in advance about where to use first circle, it will give a freshness and a spontaneity to our performance. The great British comedian Bob Monkhouse, known in the business as The Governor, said that the best spontaneous gags were the well-rehearsed ones. First circle in presentations or speeches works best when it has been pre-selected.

The three Rs

- Recall
- Reflection
- Reason.

There will always be moments in our presentations, speeches and other communications when we either, recall, reflect or reason. These moments are great opportunities to employ first circle of concentration. Whether we are remembering, musing or working something out we will invariably be using our first circle of concentration, and it's good to let an audience know this – it gives a natural freshness to the delivery.

This is a perfect place to introduce a great example of first circle deployment in a speech. We would like to refer to Colonel Tim Collins again. A few years ago an events company invited us to run a series of workshops for a forum of finance directors on board a cruise ship. One of the keynote speakers for the forum was Tim. He was speaking about leadership and was making comparisons between leadership in the military and leadership in business. The speech was peppered with anecdotes of incidents of good and bad leadership, and its conclusion wrestled with the concern of how many people get the leadership business so badly wrong.

This was a great example of a speech using the three Rs. Perfect application of first circle of concentration working in tandem with second and always being in third. This is what can happen when all the components of communicating with charisma fall into place, the final one being first circle of concentration. We would all like to be able to perform like Tim and maybe we can, if we master the circles of concentration.

Back on screen

Let's stay with first circle and go back to the silver screen. It's important that we can have some good visuals of first circle of concentration to relate to. If we think that second circle of concentration has a powerful effect in film-making, wait until we see what kind of impact great first circle can have on an audience.

Stolen

Good films, like good books and good speeches, are all memorable for their beginnings and their ends. One of the finest ends to a movie is in *The Long Good Friday* with Bob Hoskins and Helen Mirren. A gangster film set in London in the 1970s with Bob Hoskins playing mobster Harold Shand. Hoskins spends the whole film working out who is trying to kill him and why. In the final scene, when he thinks that things might just be getting back to normal he is bundled into the back of his own car and kidnapped by the IRA. A young Pierce Brosnan plays his IRA captor, and engages Hoskins in a steely second circle from the front seat. The scene is stolen, however, by Hoskins's riveting performance in first circle. In one of the longest single close-ups in film history the camera focuses entirely on Hoskins's look of resignation and dread as he is driven to his place of execution, and the heart-thumping music of Francis Monkman plays us out.

Here's Johnny!

Johnny Depp displays wonderful first circle in the film *Donnie Brasco*. He plays an undercover FBI agent infiltrating the mob in New York. He records all of his conversations on a small tape recorder hidden in his boot. In one scene Depp and his mob colleagues visit a Japanese restaurant where they are asked to remove their shoes. If he does this he knows that his cover will be blown, so he invents the story of being raised in an orphanage because his father was killed by the Japanese during the war. In a fit of racism the gang force the manager of the restaurant into the toilet and beat him senseless. It is a very graphic scene that is followed by an extremely still scene, where Depp is replaying the tape of the incident in his apartment. The superb choice of single close-up reveals a brilliant first circle racked with guilt and fear. This is a marvellous example of how an actor can say nothing but reveal so much.

The last farewell

Lovers of *Inspector Morse* with John Thaw will remember the final episode in the final series. In it there is a very simple scene where Morse has left the Force and is contemplating his future. A long and slow zoom finds Thaw sitting at home listening to a serene piece of classical music. With the most remarkable and spellbinding use of first circle, Thaw lets us into his thoughts about how Morse's career has ended and there are possibly some of the actor's own thoughts about the end of a long-running series coming into play too. Great stuff!

28

The focus switchers

It's easy to fool the eye but it's hard to fool the heart.

Al Pacino

So we have written, directed and starred in our own movie. We know what this focus business is all about. That may be so, but perhaps we should remind ourselves by taking a look at a few of the great movies with focus switches. When asked about favourite films a lot of people will list *The Godfather* – some will even say Godfathers 1 and 2. Both great movies with first-class scripts and direction and acted by some of America's best such as Marlon Brando, Robert de Niro, Al Pacino, Diane Keaton, Talia Shire and Robert Duval.

There is a wonderful demonstration of focus switching in *The Godfather 2* when Al Pacino is trying to stop Diane Keaton from leaving him with their two daughters. Pacino had been hoping that they would have a boy, and tells her that she will get over her recent miscarriage and be able to get back to normal and try again. Keaton informs Pacino that she did not have a miscarriage – she had an abortion because she didn't want their son to grow up in his world. The director uses a tight close-up on Pacino as he takes in this information. In a matter of a few seconds he switches rapidly back and forth between first and second circle signifying disbelief and confusion before finally exploding with anger. It is one of the most intense and gripping moments in the film, and all down to his mastery of the circles of concentration.

There are many great scenes in *Kramer vs. Kramer* with Dustin Hoffman and Meryl Streep. One of the best face-to-face scenes is when Streep returns home to say that their son belongs at home with his father and she is not going to take him with her. Streep moves between first and second circle so skilfully we know exactly what she is feeling – she is sad and frustrated but she is also racked with guilt and shame. We get all of this through her subtle yet superb use of the circles of concentration.

Focus switching can also be used to great comic effect. Hugh Grant has made himself a world expert at this. There is one rather touching scene in *Notting Hill*, however, when Grant uses focus switching to create pathos. Julia Roberts turns up at the bookshop to ask Grant for a second chance so they can carry on seeing each other. This is a very static scene where they stand a couple of metres apart and have no physical contact. Grant manages to convey that he has given this some serious thought and has decided it best that they don't see each other any more. His use of first and second tells the story in what is one of the film's best scenes. The slightly awkward switching between first and second circle has become one of Grant's trademarks, which makes his performances highly watchable. In another marvellous scene from *Notting Hill*, Julia Roberts makes terrific use of second in third when Grant proposes to her at the press conference. Two extremely talented and charismatic actors getting the very best out of the circles of concentration.

Natural additives

Standing up and speaking in front of people is an unnatural and artificial thing to do, and our audiences enjoy the artificiality of the situation. It is our job to bring some normality to the unnatural occasion. We have all heard people say 'She is such a good speaker – it was as if she was having a normal conversation with us.' If we are to give our audiences the very best we can offer, we need to embrace the first circle of concentration and make it work in all of our addresses. We should not have to search too hard to find places we can use it. There will, without doubt, be at least one of the three Rs in all of our presentations or speeches. We will always have to recall, reflect or reason with something.

In everyday conversations we use first circle naturally. In the artificial situations of our presentations and speeches many of us will not use first circle at all. That is why we must identify areas where we can inject spontaneity – making the artificial natural – the charisma way.

29

Directing the movie

I do not suppose I shall be remembered for anything. But I don't think about my work in those terms. It is just as vulgar to work for the sake of posterity as to work for the sake of money.

Orson Welles

We've done it! We have acquired the three basic shots we need to produce a good movie – the safety shot, the intimate two shot and the single close up – what more do we need? We need to bring them all together in the right measure to grip our audience and steer them through our story. We are a one-person production team. We are writer, director, producer and actor. We are ready to make and star in our film – *Charisma: This time it's personal!*

This is where you can score over the actors. You are a one-person show. Actors are often at the mercy of bad writing or bad direction or both. You have more control.

Making your entrance

The script is in its final draft. It has been learned and rehearsed and is ready to shoot. All we need to do now is decide what shots to use and when. Let's assume that we are working a large space with an audience in excess of 50 people. When we are introduced we need to enter on stage in our third circle of concentration, sending out that energy to bring all of our audience into that third circle, never letting them go until we have left the performance space.

We need to take our time. We need to let our audience take us in. We need them to engage with us visually before we begin our opening dialogue. This is the establishing safety shot. A perfectly planned scene to allow the audience to settle and gather their attention.

Perhaps we have chosen a slight moment of first circle before we say our first words, just to bring a degree of spontaneity to our opening remarks that will draw the audience in and give them confidence in our abilities as a speaker. It will relax them and make them feel at ease with us. They might feel that they are about to witness an off-the-cuff presentation, which always breeds an air of excitement. Once our audience is in this state of calm expectancy, we have them where we want them and we can go to work.

'Action!'

We now deploy our random selection second circle of concentration in a series of intimate two shots, always remembering to give an equally spread distribution throughout the space. Every two shot is held for a matter of a few seconds and is then rapidly switched. The rapidity of the distribution should not detract from the even pace of our delivery; it is simply there to share something of ourselves with our audience while keeping them in a calm and comfortable state. If we are sufficiently on top of our material we can now begin to analyse the reactions of our audience and make any appropriate adjustments to our delivery. We should now be gaining some confidence in the fact that we have, through second circle, been able to retain a good level of attention from our audience and that they are taking in what we have to say to them.

Second in third is working well and we are really getting into our stride. Time to mix it up a little. Time to use the thinking circle. We are now coming to the first point in our talk when we are ready for our single close-up. We will have already identified the pockets in our address where we need to retreat into our first circle of concentration. When we do this there will almost certainly be a natural change of pace. Let's remember that we do not have to think in silence. We can still talk in first circle, but the speed of delivery may slow down a little as it does naturally in life. This is what makes things interesting. This is what draws the audience in. We are changing down the gears and our audience are very much in for the ride. As we recall, reflect or reason in first we will be preparing to switch focus to second. This will maintain the freshness of the speech as we engage the audience with a new thought, and change our presentation with a different dynamic. As we move back up the gears perhaps we can fix a point at the back of the space for a moment of pure third! Now we're having fun!

When we are able to harness the circles of concentration and use them with confidence, we will have completed the charisma puzzle. This is when what we have to say becomes more interesting. This is when our message becomes memorable. This is when we have a performance!

What the critics say

Did our movie sound a little far-fetched? No, certainly not! What we did may not revolutionize movie history, but we definitely engaged our audience with our story. Will our movie win any Oscars? Possibly not, but it will have entertained and connected in a positive way. Do we care what the critics say? Yes, we do! It's important that our audiences leave to talk about our performance in good terms. The only way we can stand a chance at making a positive impact is to give a powerful performance, and that means understanding how to operate our own focus, and manage the focus of our audience. It means using the circles. If we do this well we will be talked about with praise. We will rise in the estimation of our peers. We will be used as examples of what is good. We will be thought of as charismatic. What more could we possibly want?

An anonymous saying goes: 'Begin low, speak slow; take fire, rise higher; when most impressed be self-possessed; at the end wax warm, and sit down in a storm.' Good enough to write on your cuff.

On the spot or in the spot?

Practise, practise, practise those circles! The more you apply them the more habitual they will become. This is the best way to boost confidence and lower anxiety. The next time your boss asks you to do his presentation for him the task may not be so daunting. They might not be your words but at least you will have a box of tricks to help you deliver them. When you have mastered the circles of concentration, short-notice speaking will not fill you with so much dread – you will be communicating with charisma.

30

Charisma and comedy

You can't stay mad at somebody who makes you laugh.

Jay Leno

There is one type of performance where it is imperative that charisma is playing its part. It is when a certain person pops up on stage or on our screens and prepares to have us rolling in the aisles. The comedian. Comedians have to tap into and develop their natural resources of appeal because if we don't like them we will not laugh at them. Tough, but true.

How often have we heard this conversation?

'I don't think he's funny.'

'Why not?'

'I just don't like him.'

The reason we smile and laugh at certain comedians is not necessarily because of what they say, but how it is said. The pitch and the tone of their voice. The pace of their delivery. The expressions and gestures used to illustrate how they feel about what they are saying and, of course, their timing. Timing is key to a comic's success, but timing will go for nothing if we do not like the person on stage. We will return to the theatre time after time to see a comedian we like, but we will never return to see one we don't like no matter how funny they might be.

Good comedians recognize how important it is to develop a style and image that will appeal. They understand that their appeal must be as broad as possible (sometimes that is dependent on the material) to reach as many people as they can. Comics are probably the most inward looking of all performers – they have to get it right. When they walk out on stage they are alone. The success of their routine is entirely down to them. There is no supporting cast. A lonely job – and evenly lonelier if the people they have come to entertain do not like them.

If you think about the comedians you like, they will have employed SSF – they must have done whether consciously or not. Their story must be a good one or we simply won't be interested. There will almost certainly be a number of stories of their life experiences they want to share with us, and they are often linked by a central theme – the governing idea. They will probably be stories that we will recognize and nod knowingly at before erupting into laughter. The classic opening line of comics of yesteryear was 'a funny thing happened to me on the way here tonight' – cue story – we knew what we were in for and there was comfort in that knowledge. Comedians will work tirelessly on getting their story right. They will even play smaller venues than they would usually, to try out material and make the necessary adjustments for when they play venues they consider to be of more importance – they need the feedback to make sure they are on the right track. It is such attention to detail and proper preparation that is the beginning of a successful act.

When we see a comedian we like they will have adopted the right level of status for the job. They will not be at the high end of the scale and push us away – they will not be at the low end and close themselves off from us. They will be accessible. They will be letting us into their world and sharing it with us. It is this type of one-to-many communication that must let the audience connect, and anything other than a mid-level status will not do it for them. Much of their material and the questions they ask will be rhetorical, but because of the openness of the performance and the rapport and relationship developed with the audience there will be moments when some of the crowd will answer back, and the comedian must be ready for that – with the put-down.

The put-down will, of course, be done at that person's expense, which sounds awful, but if the level of status is right the comedian will be able to get away with it. There may also be areas where a comedian might like to step outside that mid-level status, either to make a point or demonstrate the behaviour of someone in their story, and a good understanding of the degrees of status will help them with this style of performance.

Finally, focus. If there was ever a communicator that had to be more focused and concentrated than any other, it is the comedian. Being able to steer and manage the focus of their audiences is the comic's major skill. There will be some comedians to whom this comes naturally, but there will be a great many who have worked hard to hone this talent. A great comedian will be able to let their audience know exactly when they want them to laugh and when they want them to stop laughing so they can carry on with the performance. That timing we spoke about is all to do with focus and concentration – when is the moment right to deliver the killer punch line? Just a half beat too early or too late can mean the difference between a titter and a belly laugh.

A comic must be in the now – their focus and concentration has to be razor-sharp – if it is not they will lose the focus of their audience and have the rotten job of trying to recover it.

Good comedians will employ all three circles. They will always be in third – totally aware of those on the perimeter of the crowd. Within that third circle they will be distributing their second circle of concentration like little raindrops from the roof of the theatre, making everyone feel included and possibly afraid of being included too much! And then there's first. Because most modern-day comedians choose to use the style of observational humour they will always be reflecting, recalling, or reasoning with some personal thought or other, which is, as we know, first circle territory. This gives them the platform they need to change direction swiftly and maintain control of the focus of their audience.

If there are any budding comics reading this book we urge you to look at using the benefit of SSF to develop your style, your image, your charisma before letting yourself loose on the unsuspecting paying public!

Part
06

Communicating with charisma – Story, Status, Focus

▶Summary

Communicating with charisma is a powerful force, yet an easily grasped concept. By accepting that SSF are the main components of great communication we can all change our lives for the better. In our summing up we want to show you how the amalgamation of Story, Status and Focus brings about Credibility, Presence and Delivery – CPD. This completes the charisma recipe. Here is how it breaks down:

CPD
Credibility
Story and credibility

In any form of communication it is essential that we remain credible at all times. Many of us will have heard speeches and presentations that although slick and polished didn't quite ring true – the bell was cracked. If we don't believe the person speaking is credible we will certainly not find them in any way charismatic.

Story and status are the key components of credibility. We have said before that if you do not believe in your story then don't tell it – you will be found out. Our story is there to support us and we must believe it. If we believe in what we have to say and the construction of our message complies with everything we have previously said about storytelling, we are a long way to achieving credibility. The moment we start talking about something we do not entirely believe in, our vocal, physical and emotional status will over-compensate and betray us. When our story is supporting us as it should, we start to feel good about what we are saying, which helps with our credibility and our appeal. Get the story right!

Status and credibility

We cannot emphasize enough the importance of adopting mid-level status for effective communication. The wrong level of status will let us down. If our story is right then we will be in the right frame of mind (mental status) to bring all the good levels of status into play.

Our physical status is the first thing people will see. An open and neutral physical status will send out the message that we are comfortable and relaxed. It will, in turn, have a reassuring effect on those we are communicating with. An open and neutral physical status will also have a calming and confidence-boosting effect on us. When good physical status is operating a mid-level vocal status will easily follow – a status that is pitched confidently and strongly without being overpowering.

Now our emotional status can truthfully colour our opinion about what we have to say. We will become credible in the eyes of those around us and there will be every chance of them being receptive to what we are saying.

Story and status working hand in glove to make us credible.

Presence

Status and presence

Status and presence are two words that sound well together – indeed some might even confuse one with the other. There can be good and bad presence. Where low or high status is used, there will be bad presence. When people say, 'Wow, the speaker had great presence' it is because mid-level status has been employed. Great presence means our audience has confidence in us as a speaker and that can only be achieved by adopting mid-level status – remember anything else will close us down. Presence is what we need, but it must be the right kind of presence and only mid-level status will provide this.

Focus and presence

The right level of status has taken us where we need to be in terms of our presence – now we can make ourselves more interesting by applying focus, to enhance and maximize the impact of our presence. Back to good old Stan and the circles of concentration. We used the artist's palette analogy earlier in this book and this is the perfect moment to bring it back. Careful application of focus will bring colour and texture to the presence we have created through adopting the right level of status. The use of the three circles of concentration will bring another dimension to our presence – that's what they are there for. Focus will dictate the varying shades of colour of our presence and complete the picture – a moving image that we completely control.

Status and focus combining to create the perfect presence.

Delivery

Demosthenes (384–322 BC) was considered by Cicero to be 'the perfect orator' and the three major components of great communication he said were 'delivery, delivery and delivery!'

Story and delivery

The story is what we are delivering and it must be in good shape. It is true, of course, that the best delivery in the world will not save bad material and that is why story and delivery have to be the perfect bedfellows. When we construct our story it must always be done with our delivery in mind. This is not a story that we are simply going to read – it has to be performed – it has to be created with performance in mind. Grammar can go out of the window when we tell our stories. There isn't an audience in the world that will be interested in punctuation when it comes to the telling of a story. Any actor worth their salt will tell you that it doesn't matter how it reads – it is how it plays that is important.

Focus and delivery

What is also important is how the storyteller looks when they are telling the story and how they are working their audience. When we create our stories we should always be mindful of a seemingly random use of focus with which we need to tell those stories. This is why story and focus must work together. Focus and the use of the circles of concentration are the finishing touches to the delivery of any material. Focus will always be the icing on the cake and stories told with a lack of varying focus are incomplete.

Stories are managed with focus.

Communicating with charisma

Total performance

As the guy from the A Team used to say: 'I love it when a plan comes together!' Wouldn't it be wonderful to have a total performance? Well, we can – that's what communicating with charisma is all about – SSF equals a total performance. When story, status and focus work together to bring about credibility, presence and delivery, we have a total performance.

If we concentrate on SSF we can increase our charisma. Just look at story, status and focus – that's all you have to do. Get the story right, check the level of status, and manage focus by using the three circles. It couldn't be simpler. SSF won't necessarily turn you into the most magnetic figure in the world, but it will help you develop and enhance your charismatic appeal and make you a much better communicator.

▶ Appendix

Great speeches as examples of communicating with charisma

I've learned that people will forget what you said, people will forget what you did, but people will never forget how you made them feel.

Maya Angelou

These extracts of great speeches by some of the world's best communicators are perfect showcases for communicating with charisma

The speeches we have chosen are:

1 Martin Luther King – I have a dream
2 Queen Elizabeth I to her army at Tilbury Fort
3 Mother Teresa – Nobel Prize acceptance speech
4 John F. Kennedy – Inaugural address
5 Napoleon Bonaparte – Farewell to the Old Guard
6 Emmeline Pankhurst – Freedom or death
7 Earl Spencer – Eulogy to Diana, Princess of Wales
8 Muhammad Ali (Cassius Clay) – The legend of Cassius Clay
9 Princess Diana – Responding to land-mines
10 Anita Roddick – Trading with principles
11 Oprah Winfrey – EMMY Awards speech
12 Shirley Chisholm – Equal rights for women
13 Giuseppe Garibaldi – To his troops
14 Barack Obama – The audacity of hope

1 Martin Luther King – I have a dream

This extract is from Martin Luther King's 'I have a dream' speech. He delivered these powerful, moving words on the steps of the Lincoln Memorial in Washington on 28 August 1963 to 250,000 civil rights supporters, at the end of the 'March on Washington for Jobs and Freedom.' This has to be one of the most moving speeches of all time, with wonderful use of repetition to reinforce the message. Great geographical images of red hills, mountains and valleys mixed with human suffering. The irrepressible governing theme here is one of hope. A great showcase for the power of story and the use of emotional status.

Let us not wallow in the valley of despair, I say to you today, my friends.

And so even though we face the difficulties of today and tomorrow, I still have a dream. It is a dream deeply rooted in the American dream.

I have a dream that one day this nation will rise up and live out the true meaning of its creed: 'We hold these truths to be self-evident, that all men are created equal.'

I have a dream that one day on the red hills of Georgia, the sons of former slaves and the sons of former slave owners will be able to sit down together at the table of brotherhood.

I have a dream that one day even the state of Mississippi, a state sweltering with the heat of injustice, sweltering with the heat of oppression, will be transformed into an oasis of freedom and justice.

I have a dream that my four little children will one day live in a nation where they will not be judged by the colour of their skin but by the content of their character.

I have a *dream* today!

I have a dream that one day, down in Alabama, with its vicious racists, with its governor having his lips dripping with the words of 'interposition' and 'nullification' – one day right there in Alabama little black boys and black girls will be able to join hands with little white boys and white girls as sisters and brothers.

I have a *dream* today!

I have a dream that one day every valley shall be exalted, and every hill and mountain shall be made low, the rough places will be made plain, and the crooked places will be made straight; ...

2 Queen Elizabeth I to her army at Tilbury Fort

Queen Elizabeth I gave this speech in August 1588 to her troops at Tilbury Fort just outside London. Her army had assembled there to prepare for an expected invasion by the Spanish Armada.

This is a fabulous story of a speech and a great illustration of personal branding. Queen Elizabeth's speech is littered with evocative words like loyal, virtue, valour, honour, noble. It must have been both moving and reassuring.

My loving people, we have been persuaded by some, that are careful of our safety, to take heed how we commit ourselves to armed multitudes, for fear of treachery; but I assure you, I do not desire to live to distrust my faithful and loving people.

Let tyrants fear; I have always so behaved myself that, under God, I have placed my chiefest strength and safeguard in the loyal hearts and good will of my subjects. And therefore I am come amongst you at this time, not as for my recreation or sport, but being resolved, in the midst and heat of the battle, to live or die amongst you all; to lay down, for my God, and for my kingdom, and for my people, my honour and my blood, even the dust.

I know I have but the body of a weak and feeble woman; but I have the heart of a king, and of a king of England, too; and think foul scorn that Parma or Spain, or any prince of Europe, should dare to invade the borders of my realms: to which, rather than any dishonour should grow by me, I myself will take up arms; I myself will be your general, judge, and rewarder of every one of your virtues in the field.

I know already, by your forwardness, that you have deserved rewards and crowns; and we do assure you, on the word of a prince, they shall be duly paid you. In the mean my lieutenant general shall be in my stead, than whom never prince commanded a more noble and worthy subject; not doubting by your obedience to my general, by your concord in the camp, and by your valour in the field, we shall shortly have a famous victory over the enemies of my God, of my kingdom, and of my people.

3 Mother Teresa – Nobel Prize acceptance speech

This extract is from Mother Teresa's Nobel Prize acceptance speech which she gave in Oslo on 11 December 1979.

It's a powerful personal story of love and sharing. Although told very simply – images of 'eyes shining with hunger…' will stay with us forever. A great showcase of story and emotional status.

Some time ago in Calcutta we had great difficulty in getting sugar, and I don't know how the word got around to the children, and a little boy of four years old, Hindu boy, went home and told his parents: I will not eat sugar for three days, I will give my sugar to Mother Teresa for her children. After three days his father and mother brought him to our home. I had never met them before, and this little one could scarcely pronounce my name, but he knew exactly what he had come to do. He knew that he wanted to share his love.

And that is why I have received such a lot of love from you all. From the time that I have come here I have simply been surrounded with love, and with real, real understanding love. It could feel as if everyone in India, everyone in Africa is somebody very special to you. And I felt quite at home I was telling Sister today. I feel in the Convent with the Sisters as if I am in Calcutta with my own Sisters. So completely at home here ...

And so here I am talking with you – I want you to find the poor here, right in your own home first. And begin love there. Be that good news to your own people. And find out about your next-door-neighbour – do you know who they are? I had the most extraordinary experience with a Hindu family who had eight children. A gentleman came to our house and said: Mother Teresa, there is a family with eight children, they had not eaten for so long – do something. So I took some rice and I went there immediately. And I saw the children, their eyes shining with hunger ...

4 John F. Kennedy – Inaugural address

This extract is from President John F. Kennedy's inaugural address which he delivered in Washington on 20 January 1961. This is a very open address in every sense. It connects brilliantly well and is a superb exercise in two-way traffic. It says – yes, I'm ready to lead you – yet at the same time talks about shared responsibility with one of the most famous quotes of the twentieth century.

So let us begin anew – remembering on both sides that civility is not a sign of weakness, and sincerity is always subject to proof.

Let us never negotiate out of fear, but let us never fear to negotiate.

Let both sides explore what problems unite us instead of belabouring those problems which divide us.

Let both sides, for the first time, formulate serious and precise proposals for the inspection and control of arms, and bring the absolute power to destroy other nations under the absolute control of all nations.

Let both sides seek to invoke the wonders of science instead of its terrors. Together let us explore the stars, conquer the deserts, eradicate disease, tap the ocean depths, and encourage the arts and commerce.

Can we forge against these enemies a grand and global alliance, North and South, East and West, that can assure a more fruitful life for all mankind? Will you join in that historic effort? In the long history of the world, only a few generations have been granted the role of defending freedom in its hour of maximum danger. I do not shrink from this responsibility – I welcome it. I do not believe that any of us would exchange places with any other people or any other generation. The energy, the faith, the devotion which we bring to this endeavour will light our country and all who serve it. And the glow from that fire can truly light the world.

And so, my fellow Americans, ask not what your country can do for you; ask what you can do for your country. My fellow citizens of the world, ask not what America will do for you, but what together we can do for the freedom of man.

5 Napoleon Bonaparte – Farewell to the Old Guard

This is the speech that Napoleon Bonaparte gave on 20 April 1814 in the courtyard at Fontainebleau. He is saying farewell to the remaining faithful officers of the Old Guard after his defeat by the allies had forced him to abdicate as Emperor of France and he was about go into exile on Elba. It's a heartfelt and somewhat sad speech from one of the world's most powerful leaders of the time as he comes to terms with loss. As a study of focus, there must have been some serious first circle activity here. One can also see the areas for recall, reflection and reason.

Soldiers of my Old Guard: I bid you farewell. For twenty years I have constantly accompanied you on the road to honour and glory. In these latter times, as in the days of our prosperity, you have invariably been models of courage and fidelity.

With men such as you our cause could not be lost; but the war would have been interminable; it would have been civil war, and that would have entailed deeper misfortunes on France.

I have sacrificed all of my interests to those of the country.

I go, but you, my friends, will continue to serve France. Her happiness was my only thought. It will still be the object of my wishes. Do not regret my fate; if I have consented to survive, it is to serve your glory. I intend to write the history of the great achievements we have performed together. Adieu, my friends. Would I could press you all to my heart.

6 Emmeline Pankhurst – Freedom or death

This extract is from a speech the British suffragette Emmeline Pankhurst delivered at the Parsons Theatre in Hartford, Connecticut, on 13 November 1913. She was an inspirational speaker with a commanding presence. This is an extremely moving personal story. The image of conflict is strong and Pankhurst's own image of suffragette, soldier and convict is particularly powerful.

Mrs Hepburn, ladies and gentlemen: Many people come to Hartford to address meetings as advocates of some reform. Tonight it is not to advocate a reform that I address a meeting in Hartford.

I do not come here as an advocate, because whatever position the suffrage movement may occupy in the United States of America, in England it has passed beyond the realm of advocacy and it has entered into the sphere of practical politics. It has become the subject of revolution and civil war, and so tonight I am not here to advocate woman suffrage. American suffragists can do that very well for themselves.

I am here as a soldier who has temporarily left the field of battle in order to explain – it seems strange it should have to be explained – what civil war is like when civil war is waged by women. I am not only here as a soldier temporarily absent from the field at battle; I am here – and that, I think, is the strangest part of my coming – I am here as a person who, according to the law courts of my country, it has been decided, is of no value to the community at all: and I am adjudged because of my life to be a dangerous person, under sentence of penal servitude in a convict prison.

So you see there is some special interest in hearing so unusual a person address you. I dare say, in the minds of many of you – you will perhaps forgive me this personal touch – that I do not look either very like a soldier or very like a convict, and yet I am both.

7 Earl Spencer – Eulogy to Diana, Princess of Wales

This is an extract of the speech Earl Spencer gave on 6 September 1997 in Westminster Abbey at the funeral of his sister Diana, Princess of Wales. It is almost impossible not to be moved by these words – well chosen and deeply heartfelt. It is a cleverly crafted speech that takes us on a most extraordinary emotional journey leaving us feeling drained yet somehow uplifted – remembering that 'particular brand of magic'. A superb example of emotional status.

I stand before you today, the representative of a family in grief, in a country in mourning, before a world in shock.

We are all united, not only in our desire to pay our respects to Diana, but rather in our need to do so.

For such was her extraordinary appeal that the tens of millions of people taking part in this service all over the world, via television and radio, who never actually met her, feel that they, too, lost someone close to them in the early hours of Sunday morning. It is a more remarkable tribute to Diana than I can ever hope to offer her today.

Diana was the very essence of compassion, of duty, of style, of beauty. All over the world she was a symbol of selfless humanity, a standard-bearer for the rights of the truly downtrodden, a very British girl who transcended nationality. Someone with a natural nobility who was classless and who proved in the last year that she needed no royal title to continue to generate her particular brand of magic.

Today is our chance to say thank you for the way you brightened our lives, even though God granted you but half a life. We will all feel cheated always that you were taken from us so young, and yet we must learn to be grateful that you came along at all. Only now you are gone do we truly appreciate what we are now without, and we want you to know that life without you is very, very difficult.

We have all despaired at our loss over the past week, and only the strength of the message you gave us through your years of giving has afforded us the strength to move forward.

8 Muhammad Ali (Cassius Clay) – The legend of Cassius Clay

Boxing legend Muhammad Ali (Cassius Clay) recited this poem about himself on the Jack Paar show. He was accompanied by Liberace on the piano. Possibly the most charismatic sporting figure of all time, Ali was constantly reminding us of who he was with his almost cruel wit and repartee. This poem is typical Ali – brash, in your face but with tongue firmly in cheek! Personal branding taken to another level.

This is the legend of Cassius Clay,

The most beautiful fighter in the world today.

He talks a great deal, and brags indeed-y,

Of a muscular punch that's incredibly speed-y.

The fistic world was dull and weary,

but with a champ like Liston,

things had to be dreary.

Then someone with colour and someone with dash,

brought fight fans are runnin' with Cash.

This brash young boxer is something to see

and the heavyweight championship is his destiny.

This kid's got a left, this kid's got a right.

If he hit you once, you're asleep for the night.

9 Princess Diana – Responding to land-mines

This is an extract from the speech Princess Diana gave on 12 June 1997 at a one-day seminar hosted by the Mines Advisory Group and the Land-mine Survivors Network. The full title of the speech was 'Responding to Land-mines: A Modern Tragedy and its Solutions'. There is a humility about this speech that one cannot help be touched by. It has an honesty that draws us in. It makes us want to care

and it does that because she has decided that the only way to change the way we feel about this terrible plight is to tell us exactly how she feels about it herself. It is that emotional investment that wins through.

For the mine is a stealthy killer. Long after conflict is ended, its innocent victims die or are wounded singly, in countries of which we hear little. Their lonely fate is never reported. The world, with its many other pre-occupations, remains largely unmoved by a death roll of something like 800 people every month – many of them women and children. Those who are not killed outright – and they number another 1,200 a month – suffer terrible injuries and are handicapped for life. I was in Angola in January with the British Red Cross – a country where there are 15 million land-mines in a population, ladies and gentlemen, of 10 million – with the desire of drawing world attention to this vital, but hitherto largely neglected issue.

… I am not a political figure. As I said at the time, and I'd like to reiterate now, my interests are humanitarian. That is why I felt drawn to this human tragedy. This is why I wanted to play down my part in working towards a world-wide ban on these weapons. During my days in Angola, I saw at first-hand three aspects of this scourge. In the hospitals of Luanda, the capital, and Huambo, scene of bitter fighting not long ago, I visited some of the mine victims who had survived, and saw their injuries. I am not going to describe them, because in my experience it turns too many people away from the subject. Suffice to say, that when you look at the mangled bodies, some of them children, caught by these mines, you marvel at their survival. What is so cruel about these injuries, is that they are almost invariably suffered where medical resources are scarce.

10 Anita Roddick – Trading with principles

*This is an extract of the speech Anita Roddick gave to
the International Forum on Globalization's Tech-In at
Seattle, on 27 November 1999. As a very successful busi-
nesswoman, human rights activist and environmental
campaigner she fought hard for fair trade and ethical con-
sumerism. Roddick had a great story to tell and in this
speech she has clearly made decisions about how she wants
people to feel with this scary, almost futuristic imagery of
'gleaming towers of high finance' and 'out of control global
casinos' juxtaposed with gritty, evocative phrases such as
'reducing powerless communities access to basic human
rights.' It's a great speech.*

We are in Seattle arguing for a world trade system
that puts basic human rights and the environment at
its core. We have the most powerful corporations of
the world ranged against us. They own the media that
informs us – or fails to inform us. And they probably
own the politicians too. It's enough to make anybody
feel a little edgy.

So here's a question for the world trade negotiators.
Who is the system you are lavishing so much attention on supposed to serve?

We can ask the same question of the gleaming
towers of Wall Street or the City of London – and
the powerful men and women who tinker with the
money system which drives world trade. Who is this
system for?

Let's look more closely. Every day, the gleaming towers of high finance oversee a global flow of two trillion
dollars through their computer screens. And the terrifying thing is that only three per cent of that – that's
three hundredths – has anything to do with trade at
all. Let alone free trade between equal communities.

It has everything to do with money. The great global myth being that the current world trade system is for anything but money.

The other 97 per cent of the two trillion is speculation. It is froth – but froth with terrifying power over people's lives. Reducing powerless communities access to basic human rights can make money, but not for them. But then the system isn't designed for them.

It isn't designed for you and me either. We all of us, rich and poor, have to live with the insecurity caused by an out of control global casino with a built-in bias towards instability. Because it is instability that makes money for the money-traders.

11 Oprah Winfrey – EMMY Awards speech

This is an extract of the speech Oprah Winfrey gave at the 54th Annual EMMY Awards on 22 September 2002 on receiving the first Bob Hope Humanitarian Award. This is a simple story with a big message, and the use of names creates for us an image that re-enforces the human element of that story. Oh to be around that table breaking bread with Fox and Shorty and Bootsy and Slim! A personal story that resonates.

I grew up in Nashville with a father who owned a barbershop, Winfrey's Barber Shop, he still does, I can't get him to retire. And every holiday, every holiday, all of the transients and the guys who I thought were just losers who hung out at the shop, and were always bumming haircuts from my father and borrowing money from my dad, all those guys always ended up at our dinner table. They were a cast of real characters – it was Fox and Shorty and Bootsy and Slim. And I would say, 'Bootsy, could you pass the peas please?' And I would often say to my father afterwards, 'Dad, why can't we just have regular people at our Christmas dinner?' – because I was looking for the Currier & Ives version. And my father said to me, 'They are regular people. They're just like you. They want the same thing you want.' And I would say, 'What?' And he'd say, 'To be fed.' And at the time, I just thought he was talking about dinner. But I have since learned how profound he really was, because we all are just regular people seeking the same thing. The guy on the street, the woman in the classroom, the Israeli, the Afghani, the Zuni, the Apache, the Irish, the Protestant, the Catholic, the gay, the straight, you, me – we all just want to know that we matter. We want validation. We want the same things. We want safety and we want to live a long life. We want to find somebody to love … We want to find somebody to laugh with and have the power and the place to cry with when necessary.

… What I've learned is that we all just want to be heard.

12 Shirley Chisholm – Equal rights for women

This is an extract of the address Shirley Chisholm delivered to The United States House Of Representatives, Washington, DC on 21 May 1969. She was the first black congresswoman and the first African-American woman to seek nomination for the presidency. This is a story of struggle and repression. Chisholm was clearly and quite rightly influenced by Pankhurst and Martin Luther King. It is a good story that was well told with strength, passion and hope as a catalyst for change.

Mr Speaker, when a young woman graduates from college and starts looking for a job, she is likely to have a frustrating and even demeaning experience ahead of her. If she walks into an office for an interview, the first question she will be asked is, 'Do you type?'

There is a calculated system of prejudice that lies unspoken behind that question. Why is it acceptable for women to be secretaries, librarians, and teachers, but totally unacceptable for them to be managers, administrators, doctors, lawyers, and members of Congress?

The unspoken assumption is that women are different. They do not have executive ability orderly minds, stability, leadership skills, and they are too emotional.

It has been observed before, that society for a long time discriminated against another minority, the blacks, on the same basis – that they were different and inferior. The happy little homemaker and the contented 'old darkey' on the plantation were both produced by prejudice.

As a black person, I am no stranger to race prejudice. But the truth is that in the political world I have been far oftener discriminated against because I am a woman than because I am black.

Prejudice against blacks is becoming unacceptable although it will take years to eliminate it. But it is doomed because, slowly, white America is beginning to admit that it exists. Prejudice against women is still acceptable. There is very little understanding yet of the immorality involved in double pay scales and the classification of most of the better jobs as 'for men only'.

More than half of the population of the United States is female. But women occupy only two per cent of the managerial positions. They have not even reached the level of tokenism yet.

13 Giuseppe Garibaldi – To his troops

This is an extract of the speech the Italian military leader Giuseppe Garibaldi delivered to his soldiers in 1860, as part of his campaign to free his people from foreign rule and unify the country. A real rabble-rouser of a speech full of passion, and high in drama. If this were in a film it would be one of those major pivotal moments of the script. We particularly like the image of 'a sharpened sword forged from the links of his fetters!' Superb emotional status.

We must now consider the period which is just drawing to a close as almost the last stage of our national resurrection, and prepare ourselves to finish worthily the marvellous design of the elect of twenty generations, the completion of which providence has reserved for this fortunate age.

Yes, young men, Italy owes to you an undertaking which has merited the applause of the universe. You have conquered and you will conquer still, because you are prepared for the tactics that decide the fate of battles. You are not unworthy of the men who entered the ranks of a Macedonian phalanx, and who contended not in vain with the proud conquerors of Asia. To this wonderful page in our country's history another more glorious still will be added, and the slave shall show at last to his free brothers a sharpened sword forged from the links of his fetters.

To arms, then, all of you! All of you! And the oppressors and the mighty shall disappear like dust. You, too, women, cast away all the cowards from your embraces; they will give you only cowards for children, and you who are the daughters of the land of beauty must bear children who are noble and brave. Let timid doctrinaires depart from among us to carry their servility and their miserable fears elsewhere. This people is its own master. It wishes to be the brother of other peoples, but to look on the insolent with a proud glance, not to grovel before them imploring its own freedom.

It will no longer follow in the trail of men whose hearts are foul. No! No! No!

Providence has presented Italy with Victor Emmanuel. Every Italian should rally round him. By the side of Victor Emmanuel every quarrel should be forgotten …

14 Barack Obama – The audacity of hope

This is an extract of the address Illinois Senate candidate Barack Obama delivered to the Democratic National Convention in Boston on 27 July 2004.

A moving speech intended to raise spirits and confirm that anything is possible if we believe in it. Wonderful images of songs being sung around fires, and great metaphorical images of 'crossroads of history' and a 'righteous wind'. This great personal story cannot help but evoke the feeling of hope that is his intention.

I stand here today, grateful for the diversity of my heritage, aware that my parents' dreams live on in my two precious daughters. I stand here knowing that my story is part of the larger American story, that I owe a debt to all of those who came before me, and that in no other country on Earth is my story even possible …

Well, I say to them tonight, there is not a liberal America and a conservative America – there is the United States of America. There is not a black America and a white America and Latino America and Asian America – there's the United States of America …

It's the hope of slaves sitting around a fire singing freedom songs; the hope of immigrants setting out for distant shores; the hope of a young naval lieutenant bravely patrolling the Mekong Delta; the hope of a millworker's son who dares to defy the odds; the hope of a skinny kid with a funny name who believes that America has a place for him, too.

Hope! Hope in the face of difficulty. Hope in the face of uncertainty. The audacity of hope!

In the end, that is God's greatest gift to us, the bedrock of this nation. A belief in things not seen. A belief that there are better days ahead.

I believe that we can give our middle-class relief and provide working families with a road to opportunity.

I believe we can provide jobs to the jobless, homes to the homeless, and reclaim young people in cities across America from violence and despair.

I believe that we have a righteous wind at our backs and that as we stand on the crossroads of history, we can make the right choices, and meet the challenges that face us.

We include the four following speeches in full as examples of great communication on every level:

15 Winston Churchill – We shall fight on the beaches

16 John F. Kennedy – Ich bin ein Berliner

17 Lieutenant-Colonel Tim Collins – Magnanimous in victory

18 Bill Clinton – I believe in a place called hope

15 Winston Churchill – We shall fight on the beaches

Winston Churchill gave this speech on 4 June 1940 to the House of Commons. Although often known as 'We shall fight them on the beaches' this is in fact a misquotation of 'We shall fight on the beaches.'

As well as using the techniques of story and structure that we have discussed in the book, it also of course uses anaphora – the technique where a word or phrase is emphasized by it being repeated at the beginning of successive clauses or sentences – 'We shall fight ...'

Turning once again, and this time more generally, to the question of invasion, I would observe that there has never been a period in all these long centuries of which we boast when an absolute guarantee against invasion, still less against serious raids, could have been given to our people.

In the days of Napoleon the same wind which would have carried his transports across the Channel might have driven away the blockading fleet. There was always the chance, and it is that chance which has excited and befooled the imaginations of many Continental tyrants.

Many are the tales that are told. We are assured that novel methods will be adopted, and when we see the originality of malice, the ingenuity of aggression, which our enemy displays, we may certainly prepare ourselves for every kind of novel stratagem and every kind of brutal and treacherous manoeuvre. I think that no idea is so outlandish that it should not be considered and viewed with a searching, but at the same time, I hope, with a steady eye. We must never forget the solid assurances of sea power and those which belong to air power if it can be locally exercised.

I have, myself, full confidence that if all do their duty, if nothing is neglected, and if the best arrangements are made, as they are being made, we shall prove ourselves once again able to defend our Island home, to ride out the storm of war, and to outlive the menace of tyranny, if necessary for years, if necessary alone.

At any rate, that is what we are going to try to do. That is the resolve of His Majesty's Government – every man of them. That is the will of Parliament and the nation.

The British Empire and the French Republic, linked together in their cause and in their need, will defend to the death their native soil, aiding each other like good comrades to the utmost of their strength.

Even though large tracts of Europe and many old and famous states have fallen or may fall into the grip of the Gestapo and all the odious apparatus of Nazi rule, we shall not flag or fail.

We shall go on to the end, we shall fight in France,

we shall fight on the seas and oceans,

we shall fight with growing confidence and growing strength in the air, we shall defend our Island, whatever the cost may be,

we shall fight on the beaches,

we shall fight on the landing grounds,

we shall fight in the fields and in the streets,

we shall fight in the hills,

we shall never surrender; and even if, which I do not for a moment believe, this Island or a large part of it were subjugated and starving, then our Empire beyond the seas, armed and guarded by the British Fleet, would carry on the struggle, until, in God's good time, the New World, with all its power and might, steps forth to the rescue and the liberation of the old.

Reproduced with permission of Curtis Brown Ltd, London on behalf of The Estate of Winston Churchill

President Kennedy gave this speech in Berlin on 26 June 1963. His audience was a crowd in the Rudolph Wilde Platz near the Berlin Wall.

I am proud to come to this city as the guest of your distinguished Mayor, who has symbolized throughout the world the fighting spirit of West Berlin. And I am proud to visit the Federal Republic with your distinguished Chancellor who for so many years has committed Germany to democracy and freedom and progress, and to come here in the company of my fellow American, General Clay, who has been in this city during its great moments of crisis and will come again if ever needed.

Two thousand years ago the proudest boast was 'civis Romanus sum'. Today, in the world of freedom, the proudest boast is 'Ich bin ein Berliner'.

I appreciate my interpreter translating my German!

There are many people in the world who really don't understand, or say they don't, what is the great issue between the free world and the communist world. Let them come to Berlin. There are some who say that communism is the wave of the future. Let them come to Berlin. And there are some who say in Europe and elsewhere we can work with the communists. Let them come to Berlin. And there are even a few who say that it is true that communism is an evil system, but it permits us to make economic progress. Lass' sie nach Berlin kommen. Let them come to Berlin.

Freedom has many difficulties and democracy is not perfect, but we have never had to put a wall up to keep our people in, to prevent them from leaving us. I want to say, on behalf of my countrymen, who live many miles away on the other side of the Atlantic, who are far distant from you, that they take the greatest pride that they have been able to share with you, even from a distance, the story of the last 18 years. I know of no town, no city, that has been besieged for 18 years that still lives with the vitality and the force, and the hope and the determination of the city of West Berlin. While the wall is the most obvious and vivid demonstration of the failures of the communist system, for all the world to see, we take no satisfaction in it, for it is, as your Mayor has said, an offence not only against history but an offence against humanity, separating families, dividing husbands and wives and brothers and sisters, and dividing a people who wish to be joined together.

What is true of this city is true of Germany – real, lasting peace in Europe can never be assured as long as one German out of four is denied the elementary right of free men, and that is to make a free choice. In 18 years of peace and good faith, this generation of Germans has earned the right to be free, including the right to unite their families and their nation in lasting peace, with good will to all people. You live in a defended island of freedom, but your life is part of the main. So let me ask you as I close, to lift your eyes beyond the dangers of today, to the hopes of tomorrow, beyond the freedom merely of this city of Berlin, or your country of Germany, to the advance of freedom everywhere, beyond the wall to the day of peace with justice, beyond yourselves and ourselves to all mankind.

Freedom is indivisible, and when one man is enslaved, all are not free. When all are free, then we can look forward to that day when this city will be joined as one and this country and this great Continent of Europe in a peaceful and hopeful globe. When that day finally comes, as it will, the people of West Berlin can take sober satisfaction in the fact that they were in the front lines for almost two decades.

All free men, wherever they may live, are citizens of Berlin, and, therefore, as a free man, I take pride in the words 'Ich bin ein Berliner'.

17 Lieutenant-Colonel Tim Collins – Magnanimous in victory

This is the speech that Lieutenant-Colonel Tim Collins gave the battlegroup of the 1st Battalion of the Royal Irish Regiment at the Mayne desert camp, 20 miles from the Iraqi border. The US deadline for Saddam Hussein to leave Iraq or face military action was fast approaching.

We go to liberate, not to conquer.

We will not fly our flags in their country.

We are entering Iraq to free a people and the only flag which will be flown in that ancient land is their own.

Show respect for them.

There are some who are alive at this moment who will not be alive shortly.

Those who do not wish to go on that journey, we will not send.

As for the others, I expect you to rock their world.

Wipe them out if that is what they choose.

But if you are ferocious in battle remember to be magnanimous in victory.

Iraq is steeped in history.

It is the site of the Garden of Eden, of the Great Flood and the birthplace of Abraham.

Tread lightly there.

You will see things that no man could pay to see

— and you will have to go a long way to find a more decent, generous and upright people than the Iraqis.

You will be embarrassed by their hospitality even though they have nothing.

Don't treat them as refugees for they are in their own country.

Their children will be poor, in years to come they will know that the light of liberation in their lives was brought by you.

If there are casualties of war then remember that when they woke up and got dressed in the morning they did not plan to die this day.

Allow them dignity in death.

Bury them properly and mark their graves.

It is my foremost intention to bring every single one of you out alive.

But there may be people among us who will not see the end of this campaign.

We will put them in their sleeping bags and send them back.

There will be no time for sorrow.

The enemy should be in no doubt that we are his nemesis and that we are bringing about his rightful destruction.

There are many regional commanders who have stains on their souls and they are stoking the fires of hell for Saddam.

He and his forces will be destroyed by this coalition for what they have done.

As they die they will know their deeds have brought them to this place. Show them no pity.

It is a big step to take another human life.

It is not to be done lightly.

I know of men who have taken life needlessly in other conflicts.

I can assure you they live with the mark of Cain upon them.

If someone surrenders to you then remember they have that right in international law and ensure that one day they go home to their family.

The ones who wish to fight, well, we aim to please.

If you harm the regiment or its history by over-enthusiasm in killing or in cowardice, know it is your family who will suffer.

You will be shunned unless your conduct is of the highest – for your deeds will follow you down through history.

We will bring shame on neither our uniform or our nation.

It is not a question of if, it's a question of when.

We know he has already devolved the decision to lower commanders, and that means he has already taken the decision himself.

If we survive the first strike we will survive the attack.

As for ourselves, let's bring everyone home and leave Iraq a better place for us having been there.

Our business now is North.

18 Bill Clinton – I believe in a place called hope

As someone widely recognized as one of the world's greatest communicators we conclude this book with one of Bill Clinton's finest speeches. This is the speech he gave accepting the presidential nomination at the Democratic

National Convention in New York 1992. It's a passionate speech about hope for the future in which we see a consummate performer using his communication abilities to the full. Full of spontaneity and life, using emotional status to enormous effect yet still remaining in the 5–7 charisma channel. Bright and energetic with a great distribution of personal focus. There's a mastery of rhetoric and superb use of story. There are also some great moments where Clinton tells the audience his 'story of me'.

Governor Richards, Chairman Brown, Mayor Dinkins, our great host, and my fellow Americans.

I am so proud of Al Gore. He said he came here tonight because he always wanted to do the warm-up for Elvis. Well, I ran for president this year for one reason and one reason only: I wanted to come back to this convention centre and finish that speech I started four years ago.

Well, last night Mario Cuomo taught us how a real nominating speech should be given. He also made it clear why we have to steer our ship of state on a new course.

Tonight I want to talk with you about my hope for the future, my faith in the American people, and my vision of the kind of country we can build, together.

I salute the good men who were my companions on the campaign trail: Tom Harkin, Bob Kerrey, Doug Wilder, Jerry Brown and Paul Tsongas. One sentence in the platform we built says it all: 'The most important family policy, urban policy, labour policy, minority policy and foreign policy America can have is an expanding, entrepreneurial economy of high-wage, high-skill jobs.'

And so, in the name of all the people who do the work, pay the taxes, raise the kids and play by the rules, in the name of the hard-working Americans who make up our forgotten middle class, I accept your nomination for President of the United States.

I am a product of that middle class. And when I am President you will be forgotten no more.

We meet at a special moment in history, you and I. The Cold War is over; Soviet Communism has collapsed; and our values – freedom, democracy, individual rights and free enterprise – they have triumphed all around the world. And yet just as we have won the Cold War abroad, we are losing the battles for economic opportunity and social justice here at home. Now that we have changed the world, it's time to change America.

I have news for the forces of greed and the defenders of the status quo: your time has come – and gone. It's time for a change in America.

Tonight ten million of our fellow Americans are out of work. Tens of millions more work harder for lower pay. The incumbent president says unemployment always goes up a little before a recovery begins. But unemployment only has to go up by one more person before a real recovery can begin. And, Mr President, you are that man.

This election is about putting power back in your hands and putting government back on your side. It's about putting people first.

You know, I've said that all across the country, and someone always comes back at me, as a young man did just this week at the Henry Street Settlement on the Lower East Side of Manhattan. He said, 'That sounds good, Bill. But you're a politician. Why should I trust you?'

Tonight, as plainly as I can, I want to tell you who I am, what I believe, and where I want to lead America.

I never met my father. He was killed in a car wreck on a rainy road three months before I was born, driving home from Chicago to Arkansas to see my mother.

After that, my mother had to support us. So we lived with my grandparents while she went back to Louisiana to study nursing.

I can still see her clearly tonight through the eyes of a three-year-old: kneeling at the railroad station and weeping as she put me back on the train to Arkansas with my grandmother. She endured her pain because she knew her sacrifice was the only way she could support me and give me a better life.

My mother taught me. She taught me about family and hard work and sacrifice. She held steady through tragedy after tragedy. And she held our family, my brother and I, together through tough times. As a child, I watched her go off to work each day at a time when it wasn't always easy to be a working mother.

As an adult, I've watched her fight off breast cancer. And again she has taught me a lesson in courage. And always, always she taught me to fight.

That's why I'll fight to create high-paying jobs so that parents can afford to raise their children today. That's why I'm so committed to making sure every American gets the health care that saved my mother's life, and that women's health care gets the same attention as men's. That's why I'll fight to make sure women in this country receive respect and dignity – whether they work in the home, out of the home, or both. You want to know where I get my fighting spirit? It all started with my mother.

Thank you, Mother. I love you.

When I think about opportunity for all Americans, I think about my grandfather.

He ran a country store in our little town of Hope. There were no food stamps back then, so when his customers – whether they were white or black, who worked hard and did the best they could, came in with no money – well, he gave them food anyway – just made a note of it. So did I. Before I was big enough to see over the counter, I learned from him to look up to people other folks looked down on.

My grandfather just had a grade-school education. But in that country store he taught me more about equality in the eyes of the Lord than all my professors at Georgetown; more about the intrinsic worth of every individual than all the philosophers at Oxford; and he taught me more about the need for equal justice than all the jurists at Yale Law School.

If you want to know where I come by the passionate commitment I have to bringing people together without regard to race, it all started with my grandfather.

I learned a lot from another person, too. A person who for more than 20 years has worked hard to help our children – paying the price of time to make sure our schools don't fail them. Someone who travelled our state for a year, studying, learning, listening, going to PTA meetings, school board meetings, town hall meetings, putting together a package of school reforms recognized around the nation, and doing it all while building a distinguished legal career and being a wonderful loving mother.

That person is my wife.

Hillary taught me. She taught me that all children can learn, and that each of us has a duty to help them do it. So if you want to know why I care so much about our children and our future; it all started with Hillary. I love you.

Frankly, I'm fed up with politicians in Washington lecturing the rest of us about 'family values'. Our families have values. But our government doesn't.

I want an America where 'family values' live in our actions, not just in our speeches – an America that includes every family, every traditional family and every extended family, every two-parent family, every single-parent family, and every foster family – every family.

I do want to say something to the fathers in this country who have chosen to abandon their children by neglecting to pay their child support: take responsibility for your children or we will force you to do so. Because governments don't raise children; parents do. And you should.

And I want to say something to every child in America tonight who is out there trying to grow up without a father or a mother: I know how you feel. You're special, too. You matter to America. And don't ever let anybody tell you you can't become whatever you want to be. And if other politicians make you feel like you're not a part of their family, come on and be part of ours.

The thing that makes me angriest about what's gone wrong in the last 12 years is that our government has lost touch with our values, while our politicians continue to shout about them. I'm tired of it.

I was raised to believe its that the American Dream was built on rewarding hard work. But we have seen the folks in Washington turn the American ethic on its head. For too long, those who play by the rules and keep the faith have gotten the shaft, and those who cut corners and cut deals have been rewarded. People are working harder than ever, spending less time with their children, working nights and weekends at their jobs instead of gong to PTA and Little League or Scouts, and their incomes are still going down. Their taxes are going up, and the costs of health care, housing and education are going through the roof. Meanwhile, more and more of our best people are falling into poverty – even when they work forty hours a week.

Our people are pleading for change, but government is in the way. It has been hijacked by privileged, private interests. It has forgotten who really pays the bills around here – it's taking more of your money and giving you less in return.

We have got to go beyond the brain-dead politics in Washington, and give our people the kind of government they deserve: a government that works for them.

A president – a president ought to be a powerful force for progress. But right now I know how President Lincoln felt when General McClellan wouldn't attack in the Civil War. He asked him, 'If you're not going to use your army, may I borrow it?' And so I say, George Bush, if you won't use your power to help America, step aside. I will.

Our country is falling behind. The President is caught in the grip of a failed economic theory. We have gone from first to thirteenth in the world in wages since Reagan and Bush have been in office. Four years ago, candidate Bush said America is a special place, not just 'another pleasant country on the UN roll call, between Albania and Zimbabwe.' Now, under President Bush, America has an unpleasant economy stuck somewhere between Germany and Sri Lanka. And for most Americans, Mr President, life's a lot less kind and a lot less gentle than it was before your administration took office.

Our country has fallen so far, so fast that just a few months ago the Japanese Prime Minister actually said he felt 'sympathy' for the United States. Sympathy. When I am your president, the rest of the world will not look down on us with pity, but up to us with respect again.

What is George Bush doing about our economic problems? Now, four years ago he promised us fifteen million new jobs by this time. And he's over fourteen million short. Al Gore and I can do better.

He has raised taxes on the people driving pick-up trucks, and lowered taxes on people riding in limousines. We can do better.

He promised to balance the budget, but he hasn't even tried. In fact, the budgets he has submitted have nearly doubled the debt. Even worse, he wasted billions and reduced our investment in education and jobs. We can do better.

So if you are sick and tired of a government that doesn't work to create jobs; if you're sick and tired of a tax system that's stacked against you; if you're sick and tired of exploding debt and reduced investments in our future – or if, like the great civil rights pioneer Fannie Lou Hamer, you're just plain old sick and tired of being sick and tired – then join us, work with us, win with us. And we can make our country the country it was meant to be.

Now, George Bush talks a good game. But he has no game plan to rebuild America from the cities to the suburbs to the countryside so that we can compete and win again in the global economy. I do.

He won't take on the big insurance companies and the bureaucracies to control health costs and give us affordable health care for all Americans. But I will.

He won't even implement the recommendations of his own commission on AIDS. But I will.

He won't streamline the Federal Government, and change the way it works; cut a hundred thousand bureaucrats, and put a hundred thousand new police officers on the streets of American cities. But I will.

He has never balanced a government budget. But I have, eleven times.

He won't break the stranglehold the special interests have on our elections and the lobbyists have on our government. But I will.

He won't give mothers and fathers the simple chance to take some time off from work when a baby is born or a parent is sick. But I will.

We're losing our family farms at a rapid rate, and he has no commitment to keep family farms in the family. But I do.

He's talked a lot about drugs, but he hasn't helped people on the front line to wage that war on drugs and crime. But I will.

He won't take the lead in protecting the environment and creating new jobs in environmental technology. But I will.

You know what else? He doesn't have Al Gore and I do.

Just in case – just in case you didn't notice, that's Gore with an E on the end.

And George Bush – George Bush won't guarantee a woman's right to choose. I will. Listen, hear me now: I am not pro-abortion. I am pro-choice strongly. I believe this difficult and painful decision should be left to the women of America. I hope the right to privacy can be protected, and we will never again have to discuss this issue on political platforms. But I am old enough to remember what it was like before Roe v. Wade. And I do not want to return to the time when we made criminals of women and their doctors.

Jobs. Education. Health care. These are not just commitments from my lips. They are the work of my life.

Our priorities must be clear: we will put our people first again. But priorities without a clear plan of action are just empty words. To turn our rhetoric into reality we've got to change the way government does business – fundamentally. Until we do, we'll continue to pour billions of dollars down the drain.

The Republicans have campaigned against big government for a generation. But have you noticed? They've run this big government for a generation. And they haven't changed a thing. They don't want to fix government. They still want to campaign against it, and that's all.

But, my fellow Democrats, it's time for us to realize that we've got some changing to do too. There is not a programme in government for every problem. And if we want to use government to help people, we've got to make it work again.

Because we are committed in this convention and in this platform to making these changes, we are, as Democrats, in the words that Ross Perot himself spoke today, a revitalized Democratic party. I am well aware that all those millions of people who rallied to Ross Perot's cause wanted to be in an army of patriots for change. Tonight I say to them: join us and together we will revitalize America.

Now, I don't have all the answers. But I do know the old ways don't work. Trickle-down economics has sure failed. And big bureaucracies, both private and public, they've failed, too.

That's why we need a new approach to government – a government that offers more empowerment and less entitlement, more choices for young people in the schools they attend, in the public schools they attend, and more choices for the elderly and for people with disabilities and the long-term care they receive – a government that is leaner, not meaner. A government that expands opportunity, not bureaucracy – a government that understands that jobs must come from growth in a vibrant and vital system of free enterprise. I call this approach a New Covenant – a solemn agreement between the people and their government – based not simply on what each of us can take but on what all of us must give to our nation.

We offer our people a new choice based on old values. We offer opportunity. We demand responsibility. We will build an American community again. The choice we offer is not conservative or liberal. In many ways it's not even Republican or Democratic, It's different. It's new. And it will work.

It will work because it is rooted in the vision and the values of the American people. Of all the things George Bush has ever said that I disagree with, perhaps the thing that bothers me most is how he derides and degrades the American tradition of seeing – and seeking – a better future. He mocks it as 'the vision thing'. But remember just what the Scripture says: 'Where there is no vision the people perish.' I hope – I hope nobody in this great hall tonight or in our beloved country has to go through tomorrow without a vision. I hope no one ever tries to raise a child without a vision. I hope nobody ever starts a business or plants a crop in the ground without a vision – for where there is no vision the people perish.

One of the reasons we have so many children in so much trouble in so many places in this nation is because they have seen so little opportunity, so little responsibility, and so little loving, caring community that they literally cannot imagine the life we are calling them to lead. And so I say again, where there is no vision America will perish.

What is the vision of our New Covenant?

An America with millions of new jobs in dozens of new industries moving confidently toward the twenty-first century. An America that says to entrepreneurs and business people: We will give you more incentives and more opportunity than ever before to develop the skills of your workers and create American jobs and American wealth in the new global economy. But you must do your part; you must be responsible. American companies must act like American companies again – exporting products, not jobs. That's what this New Covenant is all about.

An America in which the doors of college are thrown open once again to the sons and daughters of stenographers and steelworkers. We'll say: Everybody can borrow the money to go to college. But you must do your part. You must pay it back – from your paychecks, or better yet, by going back home and serving your communities. Just think of it. Think of it; millions of energetic young men and women, serving their country by policing the streets, or teaching the children or caring for the sick, or working with the elderly or people with disabilities, or helping young people to stay off drugs and out of gangs, giving us all a sense of new hope and limitless possibilities. That's what this New Covenant is all about.

An America in which health care is a right, not a privilege. In which we say to all of our people: Your government has the courage – finally – to take on the health care profiteers and make health care affordable for every family. But you must do your part: preventive care, prenatal care, childhood immunization; saving lives, saving money, saving families from heartbreak. That's what the New Covenant is all about.

An America in which middle class incomes – not middle class taxes – are going up. An America, yes, in which the wealthiest few – those making over $200,000 a year – are asked to pay their fair share. An America in which the rich are not soaked – but the middle class is not drowned either. Responsibility starts at the top; that's what the New Covenant is all about.

An America where we end welfare as we know it. We will say to those on welfare: you will have and you deserve the opportunity through training and education, through child care and medical coverage, to liberate yourself. But then, when you can, you must work, because welfare should be a second chance, not a way of life. That's what the New Covenant is all about.

An America with the world's strongest defence; ready and willing to use force, when necessary. An America at the forefront of the global effort to preserve and protect our common environment – and promoting global growth. An America that will not coddle tyrants, from Baghdad to Beijing. An America that champions the cause of freedom and democracy, from Eastern Europe to Southern Africa, and in our own hemisphere in Haiti and Cuba.

The end of the Cold War permits us to reduce defence spending while still maintaining the strongest defence in the world. But we must plough back every dollar of defence cuts into building American jobs right here at home. I know well that the world needs a strong America, but we have learned that strength begins at home.

But the New Covenant is about more than opportunities and responsibilities for you and your families. It's also about our common community. Tonight every one of you knows deep in your heart that we are too divided.

It is time to heal America. And so we must say to every American: look beyond the stereotypes that blind us. We need each other. All of us, we need each other. We don't have a person to waste. And yet, for too long, politicians have told the most of us that are doing all right that what's really wrong with America is the rest of us. Them. Them the minorities. Them the liberals. Them the poor. Them the homeless. Them the people with disabilities. Them the gays. We've gotten to where we've nearly them'd ourselves to death. Them, and them, and them. But this is America. There is no them; there is only us. One nation, under God, indivisible, with liberty, and justice, for all.

That is our pledge of allegiance, and that's what the New Covenant is all about.

How do I know we can come together to make change happen? Because I have seen it in my own state. In Arkansas we're working together and we're making progress. No, there is no Arkansas miracle. But there are a lot of miraculous people. And because of them, our schools are better, our wages are higher, our factories are busier, our water is cleaner, and our budget is balanced. We're moving ahead.

I wish – I wish I could say the same thing about America under the incumbent president. He took the richest country in the world and brought it down. We took one of the poorest states in America and lifted it up.

And so I say to those who would criticize Arkansas: come on down. Especially if you're from Washington – come to Arkansas. You'll see us struggling against some problems we haven't solved yet. But you'll also see a lot of great people doing amazing things. And you might even learn a thing or two.

In the end, the New Covenant simply asks us all to be Americans again – old-fashioned Americans for a new time. Opportunity. Responsibility. Community. When we pull together, America will pull ahead. Throughout the whole history of this country, we have seen time and again that when we are united, we are unstoppable. We can seize this moment, we can make it exciting and energizing and heroic to be an American again. We can renew our faith in ourselves and each other, and restore our sense of unity and community. Scripture says, our eyes have not yet seen, nor our ears heard, nor our minds imagined what we can build.

But I cannot do it alone. No president can. We must do it together. It won't be easy and it won't be quick. We didn't get into this mess overnight, and we won't get out of it overnight. But we can do it – with our commitment and our creativity and our diversity and our strength. I want every person in this hall and every citizen in this land to reach out and join us in a great new adventure to chart a bold new future.

As a teenager I heard John Kennedy's summons to citizenship. And then, as a student at Georgetown, I heard that call clarified by a professor I had, named Carroll Quigley, who said America was the greatest country in the history of the world because our people have always believed in two great ideas: first, that tomorrow can be better than today, and second, that each of us has a personal, moral responsibility to make it so.

That future entered my life the night our daughter Chelsea was born. As I stood in that delivery room, I was overcome with the thought that God had given me a blessing my own father never knew: the chance to hold my child in my arms.

Somewhere at this very moment, another child is born in America. Let it be our cause to give that child a happy home, a healthy family, a hopeful future. Let it be our cause to see that child reach the fullest of her God-given abilities. Let it be our cause that she grow up strong and secure, braced by her challenges, but never, never struggling alone; with family and friends and a faith that in America, no one is left out; no one is left behind.

Let it be our cause that when she is able, she gives something back to her children, her community, and her country. And let it be our cause to give her a country that's coming together, and moving ahead – a country of boundless hopes and endless dreams; a country that once again lifts up its people, and inspires the world.

Let that be our cause and our commitment and our New Covenant.

I end tonight where it all began for me: I still believe in a place called Hope.

Recommended reading

▶ Story

Aesop's *Fables*
Fairy Tales by the Brothers Grimm
The Greek Myths by Robert Graves
The Art Of Rhetoric by Aristotle
On the Ideal Orator by Cicero
The Seven Basic Plots: Why We Tell Stories by Christopher Booker

▶ Status and Focus

An Actor Prepares by Konstantin Stanislavski
Creating a Role by Konstantin Stanislavski
My Life in Art by Konstantin Stanislavski
Building a Character by Konstantin Stanislavski
A Dream of Passion – The Development of the Method by Lee Strasberg
Stella Adler – The Art of Acting by Stella Adler and Howard Kissel
To the Actor by Michael Chekhov
The Right to Speak: Working with the Voice by Patsy Rodenburg
Emotional Intelligence by Daniel Goleman

INDEX